PARIS

MINI MAP+GUIDE

CONTENTS

EXPERIENCE

Left: The city of Paris in springtime
Right: Classic Parisian rooftops

NEED TO KNOW

KEY TO MAIN ICONS

🗺 Map	🚋 Tram
📍 Address/Location	🚌 Bus
📞 Telephone	RER RER
🚢 Batobus	🕐 Open
Ⓜ Metro	✕ Closed
	🌐 Website

A NOTE FROM DK TRAVEL

The rate at which the world is changing is constantly keeping the DK travel team on our toes. While we've worked hard to ensure that this edition of Paris is accurate and up-to-date, we know that opening hours alter, standards shift, prices fluctuate, places close and new ones pop up in their stead. So, if you notice we've got something wrong or left something out, we want to hear about it. Please get in touch at travelguides@dk.com

DK | Penguin Random House

This edition updated by
Contributor Ruth Reisenberger

Design Gemma Doyle, Priyanka Thakur, Stuti Tiwari

Editorial Nandini Desiraju, Dharini Ganesh, Sarah Matthew, Beverly Smart, Zoë Rutland

Picture Research Manpreet Kaur, Nishwan Rasool, Virien Chopra

Jacket Design Louise Brigenshaw, Gemma Doyle

Cartography Suresh Kumar, James Macdonald

DTP Rohit Rojal, Tanveer Zaidi

Production Controller Kariss Ainsworth

Art Director Maxine Pedliham

Publishing Director Georgina Dee

Printed and bound in China

Content previously published in DK Paris (2024). This abridged edition first published in 2020

Published in Great Britain by
Dorling Kindersley Limited
20 Vauxhall Bridge Road, London SW1V 2SA

The authorised representative in the EEA is
Dorling Kindersley Verlag GmbH. Arnulfstr.
124, 80636 Munich, Germany

Published in the United States by DK Publishing,
1745 Broadway, 20th Floor, New York, NY 10019, USA

24 25 26 27 10 9 8 7 6 5 4 3 2 1

A CIP catalogue record is available
from the British Library.

A catalogue record for this book is
available from the Library of Congress.

ISBN 978-0-2417-1022-7

FSC
MIX
Paper | Supporting
responsible forestry
www.fsc.org   FSC™ C018179

This book was made with Forest Stewardship Council™ certified paper – one small step in DK's commitment to a sustainable future. Learn more at www.dk.com/uk/information/sustainability

WELCOME TO
PARIS

Sweeping, tree-lined boulevards and beautifully manicured parks. World-class museums and cutting-edge haute cuisine. The inspiration of countless artists, writers and philosophers, Paris is a city that speaks to the soul. Whatever your dream trip to Paris includes, this DK Mini Map and Guide is the perfect companion.

The birthplace of the French Revolution, Paris is steeped in history. From the Gothic magnificence of Notre-Dame, through the Second Empire opulence of the Opéra Garnier to the elegance of the Eiffel Tower, the city's landmarks are a testament to its enduring status as a political and cultural powerhouse. Art is everywhere: lose yourself in the galleries of the Louvre and marvel at the Impressionist masterpieces in the Musée d'Orsay, or visit Belleville to view the ever-changing street art on Rue Dénoyez.

Paris's food scene is equally rich, with an array of boulangeries and bistros that reflect each neighbourhood's local flavour. Stalls overflow with fresh produce at the Marché d'Aligre, while La Cuisine offers the opportunity to learn to cook your own French classics.

And if you're seeking respite from the bustle of the city, Paris offers manicured gardens, natural woodlands and seemingly endless trails in green spaces such as the Jardin du Palais-Royal and Parc Monceau. Alternatively, play *flâneur* for the day on the Seine's footpaths or shop till you drop at Paris's many flea markets and swanky department stores.

Compact enough to travel around easily, Paris can still overwhelm with the volume of attractions on offer. We've broken the city down into easily navigable chapters, highlighting each area's unmissable sights and unexpected delights. Add insider tips, a comprehensive pull-out map and a need-to-know section full of expert advice, and you've got an indispensable guidebook. Enjoy the book, and enjoy Paris.

↓ Taking a break in
↓ Jardin des Tuileries

ÎLE DE LA CITÉ AND ÎLE ST-LOUIS

Located at the heart of Paris, these islands are the ideal place to start exploring the city. Île de la Cité houses both Notre-Dame and Sainte-Chapelle, masterpieces of Gothic architecture, while Île St-Louis is full of boutiques and cafés. Former palaces – such as the royal Conciergerie, where Marie-Antoinette was held prisoner – double as administrative buildings, giving even the day-to-day a frisson of enthralling history. Both islands are an essential, and inevitable, part of a Parisian excursion.

The stunning stained-glass windows of Sainte-Chapelle
↓

NOTRE-DAME

📍 K8 🏠 Parvis Notre-Dame - Pl Jean-Paul II 75004 Ⓜ Cité 🚌 21, 38, 47, 58, 70, 72, 81, 82 Ⓜ Notre-Dame 🕐 Temporarily, check website 🌐 notredamedeparis.fr

No other building is more associated with the history of Paris than Notre-Dame (Our Lady). The "heart" of the country, both geographically and spiritually, the cathedral rises majestically at the eastern end of the Île de la Cité. A Gothic masterpiece, it was severely damaged by fire in 2019 – including the loss of its spire – and is currently closed to visitors while reconstruction is carried out.

Notre-Dame was built on the site of a Roman temple. After Pope Alexander III laid the first stone in 1163, an army of architects and craftspeople toiled for 170 years to realize Bishop Maurice de Sully's magnificent design. At the time it was finished, in about 1334, it was 130 m (430 ft) long and featured flying buttresses, a large transept, a deep choir and 69-m-(228-ft-) high towers.

    Within the cathedral's hallowed walls, kings and emperors were crowned and royal Crusaders were blessed. But Notre-Dame was also the scene of turmoil. Revolutionaries ransacked it, banished religion, changed it into a temple to the Cult of Reason, and then used it as a wine store. Napoleon restored

↑ The cathedral's legendary *chimères* (gargoyles), hiding behind a large upper gallery between the towers

religion in 1804 and architect Viollet-le-Duc later restored the building to its former glory. Tragedy struck again in 2019, however, when a devastating fire engulfed the roof of the cathedral. Following a flood of high-profile donations, French President Emmanuel Macron vowed to rebuild Notre-Dame within five years.

↑ Jean Ravy's spectacular flying buttresses at the east end of the cathedral

> After Pope Alexander III laid the foundation stone in 1163, an army of architects and craftspeople toiled for 170 years to realize Bishop Maurice de Sully's magnificent design.

EXPÉRIENCE Île de la Cité and Île St-Louis

SAINTE-CHAPELLE

📍 J7 🏠 Blvd du Palais 75001 Ⓜ Cité 🚌 21, 38, 58, 85, 96 to Île de la Cité 🚆 St-Michel Ⓜ Notre-Dame 🕐 9am-7pm daily (Oct-Mar: to 5pm) 📅 1 Jan, 1 May, 25 Dec 🌐 sainte-chapelle.fr

Ethereal and magical, Sainte-Chapelle has been hailed as one of the greatest architectural masterpieces of the Western world. In the Middle Ages, the devout likened this church to "a gateway to heaven". Today, no visitor can fail to be transported by the blaze of light created by the 15 magnificent stained-glass windows.

A Gothic Masterpiece

The chapel was built in 1248 by Louis IX to house Christ's purported Crown of Thorns (now housed in the Notre- Dame treasury). A Gothic masterpiece, its stunning stained-glass windows – the oldest extant in Paris – are separated by narrow columns that soar 15 m (50 ft) to the star-studded, vaulted roof. The windows portray over 1,000 biblical scenes, from Genesis right through to the Crucifixion, in a kaleidoscope of red, gold, green, blue and mauve. Servants and commoners worshipped in the Lower Chapel, while the Upper Chapel was reserved for the use of the king and the royal family.

ST LOUIS' RELICS

Louis IX was highly devout, and was canonized in 1297, not long after his death. In 1239, he acquired the Crown of Thorns from the Emperor of Constantinople and, in 1241, a fragment of Christ's Cross. He built this chapel as a shrine to house them. Louis paid three times more for the relics than for the construction of Sainte-Chapelle. The crown is now kept in Notre-Dame; it survived the 2019 fire.

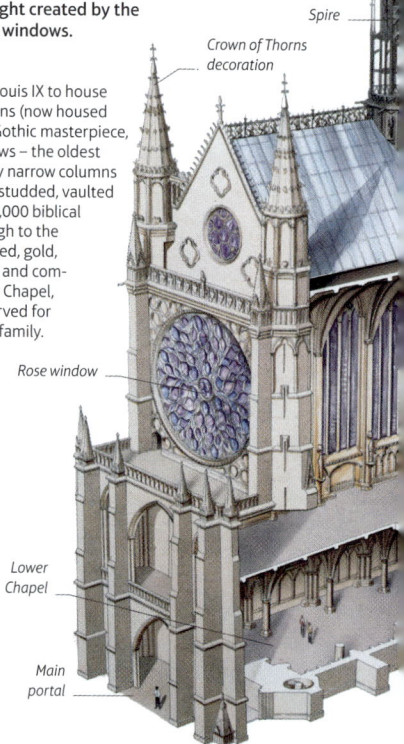

Spire

Crown of Thorns decoration

Rose window

Lower Chapel

Main portal

EXPERIENCE MORE

Angel

Upper Chapel

↑ Features of Sainte-Chapelle

Palais de Justice

📍 J7 🏠 4-10 Blvd du Palais 75001 (main entrance by the Cour de Mai, 10 Blvd du Palais) Ⓜ Cité 🕐 9am-6pm Mon-Fri 🅦 coursappel. justice.fr/paris

The monumental block of buildings stretching the entire width of the Île de la Cité was formerly the home of the central law courts, most of which have now moved into other premises in the Clichy-Batignolles quarter in the 17th arrondissement. The site, occupied since Roman times, was the seat of royal power until Charles V moved the court to the Hôtel St-Paul in the Marais during the 14th century. In April 1793, the Revolutionary Tribunal began dispensing justice from the Première Chambre, but this court eventually degenerated during Robespierre's Reign of Terror. Plans are afoot to open up more of the site to the public.

Place Dauphine

📍 J7 🏠 75001 (enter by Rue Henri-Robert) Ⓜ Pont Neuf, Cité

Southeast of Pont Neuf is this pleasant square, laid out in 1607 by Henri IV and named after the Dauphin, the future Louis XIII. It is actually triangular in shape and lined with cafés, wine bars and restaurants. In the middle is a park with trees and benches. No 14 is one of the few buildings to have avoided any subsequent restoration. This haven of 17th-century charm is popular with *pétanque* (boules) players.

Mémorial des Martyrs de la Déportation

📍 K8 🏠 Sq de l'Île de France 75004 📞 06 14 67 54 98 Ⓜ Cité, St-Paul, Maubert Mutualité, Pont Marie 🚆 St-Michel 🕐 10am-7pm daily (Oct-Mar: to 5pm) 🚫 First Mon of month, 1 Jan, 1 May, 15 Aug, 1 Nov, 25 Dec

The memorial to the 200,000 French men, women and children deported to Nazi concentration camps in World War II is covered with the names of the camps to which they were deported. Earth from these camps has been used to form tombs and the interior walls are decorated with poetry and thousands of glass crystals. At the far end is the tomb dedicated to the Unknown Deportee.

←
The old Conciergerie prison, with its turreted towers, overlooking the River Seine

Marché aux Fleurs Reine Elizabeth II

📍 K7 🏛 Pl Louis-Lépine 75004 Ⓜ Cité 🕐 9:30am-7pm Mon-Sat

Simply called Marché aux Fleurs originally, this year-round flower market was renamed in honour of Queen Elizabeth II in 2014. The market adds colour and scent to an area otherwise dominated by administrative buildings. It is the most famous and, unfortunately, one of the last remaining flower markets in the city of Paris, its attractive iron pavilions harbouring both seasonal flowers and a wide range of specialist varieties such as orchids.

Conciergerie

📍 J7 🏛 2 Blvd du Palais 75001 Ⓜ Cité 🕐 9:30am-6pm daily 🗓 1 May, 25 Dec 🌐 paris-conciergerie.fr

Part of the larger Palais de Justice, the Conciergerie, was under the administration of the palace "concierge", the keeper of the king's mansion. When the monarch moved to the Marais (in 1417), the palace remained the seat of royal administration and law; the Conciergerie became a prison, with the "concierge" as its chief gaoler. Henry IV's assassin, Ravaillac, was imprisoned and tortured here.

The Conciergerie housed more than 4,000 prisoners during the French Revolution – including Marie-Antoinette, who was held in a tiny cell, and Charlotte Corday, who stabbed Revolutionary leader Marat as he lay in his bath. Ironically, the Revolutionary judges Robespierre and Danton also became "tenants" before being sent in turn to the guillotine.

The Conciergerie has a remarkable, four-aisled Gothic Salle des Gens d'Armes (Hall of the Men-at-Arms), which serves as the dining hall for the castle's 2,000 members of staff. The building, renovated in the 19th century, also retains the 14th-century clock on the Tour de l'Horloge (Clock Tower). It is Paris's oldest public clock and is still operating.

Crypte Archéologique

📍 K8 🏛 7 Parvis Notre-Dame - Pl Jean-Paul II 75004 Ⓜ Cité, St-Michel 🕐 10am-6pm Tue-Sun 🗓 1 Jan, 1 May, 8 May, 25 Dec & religious hols 🌐 crypte.paris.fr

Situated on the main square (the *parvis*) in front of Notre-Dame and stretching 120 m (393 ft)

underground, the Crypte Archéologique exhibits the remains of foundations and walls that predate the cathedral by several hundred years. The foundations of Paris's oldest rampart, dating from the 3rd century BCE, are displayed, as are the medieval foundations of the Hôtel Dieu. Interactive touch-screens help to bring the exhibits to life.

Within the crypt are also traces of a hypocaust, a sophisticated underground heating system used for heating ancient Roman thermal baths.

Pont Neuf

9 J7 **A** Quai de la Mégisserie and Quai des Grands Augustins 75001 **M** Pont Neuf, Cité

Despite its name (New Bridge), this is the oldest of the existing bridges in Paris and has been immortalized by major literary and artistic figures since it was built. The first stone was laid by Henri III in 1578, but it was Henri IV who inaugurated it and gave it its name in 1607. His statue stands in the central section.

The bridge, which was the widest of its kind in Paris, has 12 arches and spans 275 m (912 ft). The first stone bridge in the city to be built without houses

and with pavements for pedestrians, it heralded a new era in the relationship between the Île de la Cité and the river.

From its very beginning, the Pont Neuf has had heavy traffic, and it has undergone many renovations and repairs over the centuries.

St-Louis-en-l'Île

9 L8 **A** 19 Rue St-Louis-en-l'Île 75004 **M** Pont Marie **O** 7:30am–8pm Mon–Fri, 9:30am–7pm Sat & Sun; mass: 7pm Mon–Fri, 6:30pm Sat, 11am Sun **W** saintlouisenlile.catho lique.fr

The construction of this church began in 1664 from plans by the royal architect Louis Le Vau, who lived on the island. It was completed and consecrated in 1726. Among its outstanding exterior features are the 1741 iron clock at the entrance and the pierced iron spire.

The interior, in the Baroque style, is richly decorated with gilding and marble. There is a statue of St Louis holding a Crusader's sword. A plaque in the north aisle bears the inscription "in grateful memory of St Louis in whose honour the City of St Louis, Missouri, USA is named". The church is a

popular venue for classical music concerts; details are given on the website.

Square du Vert-Galant

9 J7 **A** Île de la Cité 75001 **M** Pont Neuf, Cité

One of the most magical spots in Paris, this peaceful, tree-lined garden bears the nickname of Henri IV, "*vert-galant*". This eccentric monarch did much to beautify Paris in the early 17th century, and his popularity has lasted right up to this day. From here, there are splendid views of the Louvre and the Right Bank of the river, where Henri was assassinated in 1610. This is also the point from which the Vedettes du Pont Neuf pleasure boats depart.

EAT

Berthillon
Parisians flock to this ice-cream parlour for its unusual flavours.

9 L8 **A** 29–31 Rue St-Louis-en-l'Île 75004 **C** Mon, Tue **W** berthillon.fr.

€ € €

THE MARAIS

Full of fashionable boutiques and restaurants, the Marais is the neighbourhood visitors return to over and over again. Its noble origins are apparent in the Renaissance mansions repurposed for the likes of Chanel and the Musée Carnavalet. Along Rue des Rosiers, the scent of freshly fried falafel wafts through the air as the city's best Jewish bakeries prepare poppy-seed pastries. Parisians spend afternoons mingling at the Place des Vosges, with its lime trees set against the rosy bricks of a charming arcaded gallery.

↓ The manicured Place des Vosges

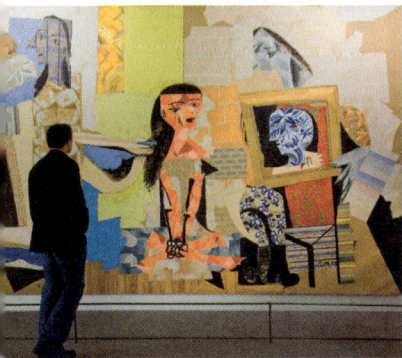

↑ A visitor contemplating Picasso's
Femmes à leur Toilette (1938)

PICASSO IN FRANCE

Born in Malaga, Spain, Picasso first visited Paris in 1900. He moved to the city in 1904, before settling in the south of France. After 1934, Picasso never returned to his homeland due to his rejection of Franco's regime. However, throughout his life in France he used Spanish themes in his art, such as the bull (often in the form of a minotaur) and the guitar, which he associated with his Andalusian childhood.

MUSÉE PICASSO PARIS

◉ M6 **⌂ Hôtel Salé, 5 Rue de Thorigny 75003** **Ⓜ St-Sébastien Froissart, St-Paul, Chemin Vert** **🚌 29, 69, 75, 96 to St-Paul, Bastille, Pl des Vosges** **🕐 10:30am-6pm Tue-Fri, 9:30am-6pm Sat & Sun; advance booking recommended** **📅 1 Jan, 1 May, 25 Dec** **🌐 museepicassoparis.fr**

The Musée Picasso Paris holds the world's largest Picasso collection. Comprising over 5,000 works and tens of thousands of archived pieces, it offers an unparalleled insight into the artist's creative process.

Spanish-born Pablo Picasso lived most of his life in France. Upon his death in 1973, the French state inherited many of his works in lieu of death duties. It used them to establish the Musée Picasso Paris, which opened in 1985. The world-renowned museum is housed in a large 17th-century mansion, the Hôtel Salé, which was built in 1656 for Aubert de Fontenay, a salt-tax collector (*salé* means "salty"). The original character of the mansion has been preserved, and large, ornate sculptures adorn the garden and courtyard. Reopened in 2014 following a five-year renovation, the museum holds works spanning a full range of media – paintings, sculptures, ceramics, drawings, etchings and drafts – covering all of Picasso's creative periods. Be sure not to miss Picasso's own collection of paintings on the third floor.

MUSÉE CARNAVALET

📍 M7 🏠 23 Rue de Sévigné Ⓜ St-Paul, Chemin Vert 🕙 10am–6pm Tue–Sun
🕙 1 Jan, 1 May 🌐 carnavalet.paris.fr

Spread across two adjoining mansions, Musée Carnavalet tells the fascinating story of Paris, from prehistoric times to the present-day. With over 618,000 items on display, this engaging museum offers it all – including temporary exhibitions and audio excerpts.

This vast museum is dedicated to the history of Paris. The Hôtel Carnavalet was built as a townhouse in 1548 by Nicolas Dupuis, and was later transformed by architect François Mansart in the 17th century. The literary hostess Madame de Sévigné lived here between 1677 and 1696, entertaining the intelligentsia of the day and writing her celebrated Lettres. Many of her belongings are displayed on the first floor.

The neighbouring 17th-century Hôtel Le Peletier de St-Fargeau, annexed to the museum in 1989 along with the Orangery, has reconstructions of early 20th-century interiors and artifacts from the Revolution and Napoleonic era. In both buildings, rooms are decorated with paintings and sculptures of prominent personalities. The collection also includes artifacts discovered in 1992, during an archaeological dig in the Parc de Bercy.

← Musée Carnavalet and its charming garden-courtyard

← A room decorated in
Chinese style, in the
Maison de Victor Hugo

are full of art galleries
and upmarket fashion
boutiques and often
ring out with the sound
of buskers playing classical music or jazz, while
at the centre of the *place*
is a beautiful formal garden with fountains and
sandpits, popular with
young families.

EXPERIENCE MORE

Maison de Victor Hugo

📍 M7 🏠 6 Pl des Vosges
75004 Ⓜ Bastille,
Chemin Vert 🕙 10am-
6pm Tue-Sun 🌐 maisons
victorhugo.paris.fr

The French poet, dramatist
and novelist lived on the
second floor of the former
Hôtel Rohan-Guéménée
from 1832 to 1848. It was
here that Victor Hugo wrote
most of *Les Misérables* and
completed many other
famous works.

The museum inside
displays reconstructions
of the rooms in which the
writer lived, his vivid pen-
and-ink drawings and cari-
catures, and books and
mementos from the cru-
cially important periods in
his life, from his childhood
to his exile between 1852
and 1870. It also holds a
number of temporary
ticketed exhibitions.

Place des Vosges

📍 M7 🏠 75003, 75004
Ⓜ Bastille, St-Paul

This square is considered
among the most beautiful
in the world by Parisians
and visitors alike. Its
impressive symmetry –
36 houses, nine on each
side, of brick and stone,
with deep slate roofs and
dormer windows over
arcades – is still intact after
400 years. It has been the
scene of many historic
events over the centuries.
A three-day tournament
was held here to celebrate
the marriage of Louis XIII
to Anne of Austria in 1615.
Cardinal Richelieu, pillar
of the monarchy, stayed
here in 1615; the famous
literary hostess Madame
de Sévigné was born here
in 1626; and the writer
Victor Hugo lived here
for 16 years. The arcades
surrounding the square

Musée Cognacq-Jay

📍 M7 🏠 Hôtel Donon,
8 Rue Elzevir 75003
Ⓜ St-Paul, Chemin Vert
🕙 10am-6pm Tue-Sun
🚫 1 Jan, Easter Mon,
1 May, 25 Dec 🌐 musee
cognacqjay.paris.fr

This small, fine collection
of 18th-century French
works of art and furniture
was formed by Ernest
Cognacq and his wife,
Louise Jay, founder of the
Art Deco La Samaritaine,
on the Quai du Louvre,
which was once Paris's
largest department
store. The collection was
bequeathed to the city
and is now housed here
in the Hôtel Donon, an
elegant building dating
from 1575 with an 18th-
century façade, wood-
panelled rooms and a
charming garden.

Pavillon de l'Arsenal

📍 M8 📌 21 Blvd Morland 75004
Ⓜ Sully Morland, Bastille
🕐 11am–7pm Tue–Sun
📅 1 Jan, 25 Dec 🌐 pavillon-arsenal.com

Dedicated to architecture and urbanism, the Pavillon de l'Arsenal organizes

SHOP

Meert

This elegant branch of the 18th-century Lillois patisserie is known for its fine vanilla-cream *gaufres* (waffles).

📍 M7 📌 16 Rue Elzévir 75003
🌐 meert.fr

Edwart Chocolatier

Gourmet chocolates with unusual flavours such as curry praline and Oolong tea are the star products at this sleek boutique.

📍 L7 📌 17 Rue Vieille du Temple 75004 🌐 edwart.fr

fascinating exhibitions throughout the year, which illustrate the architectural history and evolution of Paris. Using films, models and panoramic images, the museum explores how Paris was built over the centuries, and also gives a glimpse into future plans for the city.

Though the building dates back to 1879, inside the space feels very modern. Regular activities are held for children, and at weekends free tours are provided by architecture students (in French only).

Maison Européenne de la Photographie

📍 L7 📌 5-7 Rue de Fourcy 75004 Ⓜ St-Paul, Pont Marie 🕐 11am–8pm Wed–Sun (to 10pm Thu)
📅 1 Jan, 1 May, 25 Dec
🌐 mep-fr.org

Located in the elegant 18th-century Hôtel Hénault de Cantobre, a former private home, the Maison Européenne de la Photographie (MEP) hosts some of the best exhibitions of contemporary photography in the whole of Europe. The centre organizes cutting-edge shows alongside fascinating retrospectives on major photographers, and since opening its doors in 1996, it has hosted displays by such celebrated

photographers as Elliott Erwitt, Andy Warhol, Don McCullin, Annie Leibovitz, Robert Doisneau and Henri Cartier-Bresson. The MEP's extensive permanent collection on the history of photography is a must-see for anyone interested in exploring this medium.

Mémorial de la Shoah

📍 L7 📌 17 Rue Geoffroy-l'Asnier 75004 Ⓜ Pont Marie, St-Paul 🕐 10am–6pm Sun–Fri (to 10pm Thu); multimedia and reading rooms: 10am–5:30pm Sun–Fri (to 7:30pm Thu) 📅 Public & Jewish hols 🌐 memorialdelashoah.org

The eternal flame burning in the crypt here is the memorial to the unknown Jewish martyr of the Holocaust. Its striking feature is a large cylinder that bears the names of the concentration camps where Jewish victims of the Holocaust died. In 2005, a stone wall engraved with the names of 76,000 Jewish people – 11,000 of them children – who were deported from France to the Nazi death camps, was put up here. Various drawings, letters and artifacts from the camps are also on display, as well as photos of deportees.

every other Sunday at
pm, free guided tours
ake place in English.

Hôtel de Ville
K7 **Pl de l'Hôtel
e Ville 75004 (visitor
ntrance: 29 Rue de
ivoli, exhibitions
ntrance: 5 Rue de Lobau)**
Hôtel de Ville **Hours
ary for temporary
xhibitions** **Public
ols & official functions**
paris.fr

ome of the city council,
he town hall is a 19th-
entury reconstruction
f the original building
rected between 1533
nd 1628, which was
urned down during the
aris Commune of 1871.
is highly ornate, with
laborate stonework,
urrets and statues over-
ooking a pedestrianized
quare whose fountains
re lit up at night.

The square was
nce the main site for
angings, burnings and
ther gruesome execu-
ons. It was here that
availlac, Henri IV's
ssassin, was quartered
live in 1610, his body
pped to pieces by
ur strong horses.

Inside, the sumptuous
nction rooms – includ-
g the chandeliered Salle
es Fêtes (ballroom) – are
ostly closed to the pub-
, except on some of the

↑ Paris's imposing town
hall (Hôtel de Ville), with
its elaborate façade

Journées du Patrimoine
(Heritage Days) in Sep-
tember. The impressive
staircase, the lavish chandeliers, and the statues and
caryatids all add to the air
of ceremony and pomp here.
Free, temporary – and usually excellent – exhibitions
on Paris-related themes
are often held in the Salle
St-Jean, which is located in
the same building.

Rue des Rosiers
L7 **75004**
St-Paul, Chemin Vert
This popular pedestrianized
street is the heart of the
city's old Jewish quarter.
A Jewish community first
settled here in the 13th

century, with a second
wave of immigration
occurring in the 19th
century from Central
Europe, Poland and
Russia. Sephardic Jews
arrived from North Africa
in the 1950s and 1960s.

Around 165 students
were deported from
the nearby Jewish boys'
school, at 10 Rue des
Hospitalières-St-Gervais,
in World War II. "*N'Oubliez
pas*" (Lest we forget) is
engraved on the wall.

Most of the old Jewish
businesses have given
way to hip fashion shops,
but some – such as Sacha
Finkelsztajn bakery at
No 27 and L'As du Fallafel
at No 34 – have survived.

← Artworks on display in the Musée d'Art et d'Histoire du Judaïsme

Musée d'Art et d'Histoire du Judaïsme

📍L6 🏠Hôtel de St-Aignan, 71 Rue du Temple 75003 Ⓜ Rambuteau ⏰11am–6pm Tue–Fri (to 9pm Wed), 10am–7pm Sat & Sun 🗓1 Jan, 1 May, Rosh Hashanah & Yom Kippur 🌐mahj.org

Housed in an elegant Marais mansion, Musée d'Art et d'Histoire du Judaïsme is one of the world's leading museums on Judaism and the largest in France. Built to preserve, study and disseminate Jewish art and history, the museum commemorates the culture of French, Sephardic (Spain, Portugal, North Africa), Ashkenazi (Germany and Eastern Europe), Italian and Dutch Jewry from medieval times to the present.

There has been a sizeable Jewish community in France since Roman times, and some of the world's greatest Jewish scholars were French. Much exquisite skilfulness is showcased here, with displays of elaborate silverware and Torah covers. There are also archaeological artifacts, historical documents, photographs, paintings and cartoons.

Special exhibitions on Jewish history and contemporary politics are also organized regularly. Check the website for details and bookings.

Enceinte de Philippe Auguste

📍L7 🏠13 Rue Charlemagne 75004 Ⓜ St-Paul, Sully Morland

Dating back to 1190, these fortifications are the remains of Paris's oldest wall. King Philippe Auguste built the wall around Paris to protect the city from attacks while he was away fighting in the Crusades. A hallmark of the wall was a fortress where the Louvre now stands; its remnants are visible today in the museum's lower levels. The section here in the Marais, however, hides in plain sight. It is still possible to see the large tower, the Tour Montgomery, that formed part of the gates through which everyone had to pass in order to enter the city. The wall was an effective means of regulating trade, allowing the king to levy taxes on imports such as wine and furs, as well as many other goods.

La Cuisine Paris

📍L7 🏠80 Quai de l'Hôtel de Ville 75004 Ⓜ St-Paul 🌐lacuisineparis.com

With Paris having so many restaurants and bakeries, few visitors stop to think about learning to make their own French-inspired dishes. La Cuisine offers a variety of cooking classes run by real French cooks, who teach you how to make classic savoury dishes as well as sweet pastries in a slick kitchen offering views over the Seine. English-speaking instructors demonstrate the techniques behind buttery croissants and crusty baguettes, and demystify many of France's most iconic dishes, such as soufflés and crêpes. Some of the classes offered even combine a market visit with a cooking class where you prepare a whole lunch. After rolling up their sleeves for a few hours, La Cuisine students walk away with either a full belly or a package of flaky pastries.

The school also offers culinary walking tours of the Marais and nearby areas for visitors wanting to discover local shops and flavours. Classes and tours are open to all ages and levels of experience.

Pompidou Centre

Q K6 **A** Pl Georges Pompidou 75004 **M** Rambuteau, Châtelet, Hôtel de Ville **⏰** For renovations until 2028 **W** centrepompidou.fr

With over 120,000 works of art by more than 5,000 artists, this centre holds Europe's largest collection of modern art. In 2024, it closed for renovations; during the closure, these artworks will be displayed at the likes of the Galeries Nationales and the Louvre.

Musée de la Chasse et de la Nature

Q L6 **A** 62 Rue des Archives 75003 **M** Hôtel de Ville **⏰** 11am–6pm daily **⏰** Public hols **W** chassenature.org

The Musée de la Chasse et de la Nature (Nature and Hunting Museum) occupies the 17th-century Hôtel de Guénégaud, designed by architect François Mansart. The museum has moved away from a narrow focus on hunting to a broader, deeply emotional, reflection on humans' relationship with animals and wild spaces. Inside you'll find a fine collection of objets d'art and artworks, plus paintings by Oudry, Vernet and Rubens (including *Diane and her Nymphs Preparing to Hunt*). There are also displays of hunting weapons and stuffed animals. Temporary exhibits of contemporary art and regular cultural programmes on human-animal relationships complement the permanent collections.

Hunting artifacts showcased in Musée de la Chasse et de la Nature
↓

BASTILLE AND OBERKAMPF

Gritty and lively, these areas east of the Marais make up for a lack of major tourist attractions with stellar dining options. Trendy coffee shops, independent boutiques and innovative bars draw a younger, multicultural crowd from across the city. Flâneurs can enjoy the elevated Coulée Verte René-Dumont for a bucolic stroll above the streets, or wander the markets at Aligre and along Boulevard Richard Lenoir – both sell fresh flowers and mounds of seasonal produce. Those looking for a taste of local life will find it here.

The Bassin de l'Arsenal, a pleasure boat arena

PLACE DE LA BASTILLE

📍 N8 🏠 Place de la Bastille 75004
Ⓜ Bastille 🚍 29, 69, 76, 86, 87, 91

This busy square was the scene of one of the most important events in French history – the storming of the Bastille on 14 July 1789. Little trace of the infamous prison remains, and today the square is a hub for nightlife and cultural events such as concerts.

At the centre of the large square that marks the site of the prison is the Colonne de Juillet. Topped by the elegant, gilded statue of the winged "genius of liberty", this column of hollow bronze reaches 50.5 m (166 ft) into the sky. It is a memorial to those who died in the street battles of July 1830 that led to the overthrow of the monarch. The crypt contains the remains of 504 victims of the violent fighting and others who died in the 1848 revolution. Place de la Bastille was once the border between central Paris and the eastern *faubourgs* (working-class areas). Gentrification, however, is well under way. Just east of the Opéra Bastille is the starting point of the Coulée Verte René-Dumont, an

↑ The Colonne de Juillet in the Place de la Bastille

elevated walking trail built on a disused railway line, while the creation of a vast pedestrian plaza around the column, connected to the Bassin de l'Arsenal marina, transformed the square in 2020.

↑ The Opéra National de Paris Bastille, designed by Carlos Ott

THE FRENCH REVOLUTION

In 1789, most Parisians were living in squalor and poverty. Rising inflation and opposition to Louis XVI culminated in the storming of the Bastille, the king's prison; the Republic was founded three years later. However, the Terror soon followed, when those suspected of betraying the Revolution were executed without trial: more than 60,000 people lost their lives.

EXPERIENCE MORE

Opéra National de Paris Bastille

Q N8 **A** 120 Rue de Lyon 75012 **M** Bastille **W** operadeparis.fr

The controversial "people's opera" was officially opened on 14 July 1989 to coincide with the bicentennial celebrations of the storming of the Bastille. Carlos Ott's imposing building is a notable break with 19th-century opera-house design, epitomized by Charles Garnier's opulent Opéra in the heart of the city.

The Bastille opera house is a massive, modern, curved, glass building. The main auditorium seats an audience of 2,700; its design is functional and modern, the black upholstered seats contrasting with the granite of the walls and the impressive glass ceiling. With its five moveable stages, this opera house is certainly a masterpiece of technological wizardry and it's well worth seeing a performance here; the website has full details of what's on and also has information about guided tours (in French).

Rue de la Roquette

Q N7 **M** Bastille, Voltaire

This bustling street, lined with bars, cafés and restaurants, stretches from the Opéra Bastille towards Père Lachaise Cemetery. At No 17 stands the house of Symbolist poet Paul Verlaine, a 19th-century regular in the neighbourhood.

At No 70, a 19th-century fountain once brought water from the canal into the densely populated district. The five stone slabs in the road where the street meets Rue de la Croix Faubin are an eerie reminder of a much darker history. They are the foundations of the guillotine where inmates of the Prison de la Roquette met their fate, usually in front of a crowd of onlookers. Around 200 executions were carried out between 1851 and 1899, while some 4,000 women, members of the French Resistance, were incarcerated in the prison in 1944. The former entrance can still be seen across the street, on Square de la Roquette.

Rue de la Roquette and the surrounding area, particularly cobbled

←

Busy Rue de la Roquette with its lively cafés and restaurants

Rue de Lappe, with its numerous bars, gets pretty animated at night.

Coulée Verte René-Dumont

⊙ N8 **⌂** Ave Daumesnil 75012 **Ⓜ** Bastille **🕐** 8am-dusk Mon-Fri, 9am-dusk Sat & Sun

This former elevated railway, part of which runs along a viaduct 10 m (33 ft) above the streets, hosts Paris's most verdant walkway. The promenade, planted with many varieties of flowers and trees, stretches for about 5 km (3 miles) between the Opéra Bastille and the Périphérique city boundary to the east. The original railway closed in 1969 but the city preserved the structure and built the pretty Coulée Verte René-Dumont (also known as the Promenade Plantée) in 1993, serving as a model for urban renewal that has been replicated around the world. The topography varies from planted gardens and larger parks to narrow walkways snaking between apartment buildings. A stroll or jog along the Coulée Verte René-Dumont is a delightful traffic-free experience, with epic views of the city.

The viaduct makes up the initial stretch of the walkway. The railway arches beneath house artisan and craft shops and fashion boutiques, collectively known as the Viaduc des Arts. After 1 km (half a mile), the walkway drops to street level, continuing through residential areas, and ends near the Bois de Vincennes.

Marché d'Aligre

⊙ P8 **⌂** Place d'Aligre 75012 **Ⓜ** Ledru-Rollin **🕐** 7:30am-1:30pm Tue-Fri, 7:30am-2:30pm Sat & Sun; indoor market: 9am-1pm & 4-7:30pm Tue-Fri, 9am-1pm & 3:30-7:30pm Sat, 9am-1:30pm Sun

This lively market, with its inviting atmosphere, offers one of the most colourful sights in Paris. French, Arab and African traders hawk fruit, vegetables, flowers, clothing, bric-a-brac and second-hand books on the streets, while the adjoining covered market, the Marché Beauvau, offers fruit, vegetables, a great selection of cheese, charcuterie and olive oils, plus many intriguing international delicacies.

The Marché d'Aligre is where old and new Paris meet. Here, the established community of this old artisan quarter coexists with a more recently established group of hip urban professionals, lured here by the transformation of the nearby Bastille area. Some parts of the indoor market have been renovated following a fire in 2015.

Edith Piaf Museum

⚲ P5 ⌂ 5 Rue Crespin du Gast 75011 ☎ 01 43 55 52 72 Ⓜ Ménilmontant 🕐 1–6pm Mon–Wed; advance booking required, call ahead 🗓 Jun & Sep

Legend has it that singer Edith Piaf was born in the street in nearby Belleville. Historians debate that story, but she did actually live in this tiny apartment, now a museum dedicated to the singer's legacy. It is privately owned by a fan who has curated a collection of memorabilia and personal artifacts that belonged to the chanteuse. Just 1.42 m (4 ft 8 inches) tall and known as the "Little Sparrow", she possessed a voice that was anything but small, echoing across concert halls worldwide. Buried in nearby Père Lachaise Cemetery, Piaf is today best known for songs such as "La Vie en Rose".

An engaging collection of souvenirs, prints and Piaf's signature black dresses are on display.

> 💬 INSIDER TIP
> **Chambelland**
>
> Chambelland, at 14 Rue Ternaux, just off Rue Oberkampf, is one of the few gluten-free bakeries in Paris, serving an array of bread, biscuits and pastries.

Entry to the museum is by appointment only. A charming, intimate experience, it should appeal to both die-hard fans and visitors with just a casual interest.

Bassin de l'Arsenal

⚲ M9 ⌂ 5 Quai de la Rapée Ⓜ Bastille

Between Place de la Bastille and the Seine, this pleasure-boat arena hides below street level. A lock joins it to the River Seine. The location of a weapons storehouse since the 16th century, the arsenal eventually fell into disuse as revolutionaries removed the Bastille fortress, stone by stone.

Today, the tiny marina hosts private watercraft and is also the starting point for cruises along the Canal St-Martin. Find a spot to relax on the lawn of the pretty canalside garden where, on warm evenings, Parisians picnic along the traffic-free waterfront. Two bridges crossing the water offer picture-postcard views of the Colonne de Juillet in Place de la Bastille.

Rue Oberkampf

⚲ M6 Ⓜ Oberkampf, Parmentier

Rue Oberkampf stretches from the Upper Marais

DRINK

Moonshiner

This 1920s-inspired speakeasy hides behind a pizzeria. It can be crowded, but serves great cocktails.

⚲ N7 ⌂ 5 Rue Sedaine 75011 🌐 moonshinerbar.fr

———

La Fine Mousse

It's all about craft beer here, with up-and-coming local brews on tap. They also offer tasting workshops.

⚲ P5 ⌂ 6 Ave Jean Aicard 75011 🌐 lafinemousse.fr

———

Le Perchoir

Clink glasses and feast on light fare from this rooftop bar with a 360-degree view of the city.

⚲ P5 ⌂ 14 Rue Crespin du Gast 75011 🌐 leperchoir.fr

all the way to Ménilmontant with most of the action happening around Metros Parmentier and Oberkampf Dating back to the 1500s, the street gained its name in the 19th century from the German-born industrialist Christophe-Philippe Oberkampf, who contributed to the manufacturing of painted *toile* (French cloth).

Today, the area is anything but old-fashioned. With high-end restaurants, gourmet coffee shops, craft beer and spicy Mexican fare, Rue Oberkampf caters to all sorts of flavours and fancies in its many bars and restaurants.

The street becomes especially lively at night, with younger Parisians congregating at watering holes like Café Charbon. There are few tourist attractions here. It's all about local colour – literally, too, if you keep an eye out for the vibrant street art covering the walls and even the chimney stacks.

Spend an afternoon or evening hopping from venue to venue in search of the perfect fit.

_____

Gare de Lyon

🚇 N9 🏠 Place Louis-Armand 75012 Ⓜ Gare de Lyon Ⓦ Le Train Bleu: le-train-bleu.com

Built for the 1900 Exposition Universelle, this station is the third busiest in France, with about 110 million annual passengers. It welcomes trains from throughout France, as well as Italy, Switzerland and other international destinations. In the summer months you'll notice many sun-kissed travellers returning from the Côte d'Azur, as this station serves Nice and other southern French destinations. On the exterior of the station looms the iconic clock tower, reminiscent of the UK Parliament's Big Ben tower.

Inside the Gare de Lyon is the illustrious restaurant Le Train Bleu, a glitzy dining experience that has been in operation for over a century. The ornate dining rooms are decorated with gilded carvings, mouldings and chandeliers, as well as 41 paintings representing French cities or regions by prominent French artists including François Flameng and Henri Gervex.

Even if you're not catching a train to some sun-soaked destination, it's worth a visit to the station to sip a glass of wine amid the restaurant's sumptuous décor.

The opulent interior of Le Train Bleu restaurant, ↓ inside the Gare de Lyon

Bercy
📍 P11 🏛 75012
Ⓜ Bercy, Cour St-Émilion

This former wine-trading quarter east of the city centre, with its once-grim warehouses, pavilions and slum housing, is now a modern district. An automatic Metro line (Line 14) links it to the heart of the city. The centrepiece is the pyramidal landmark Accor Arena, which hosts a number of sports events, operas and rock concerts.

Other architecturally adventurous buildings dominate Bercy, notably Chemetov's gigantic building for the Ministry of Finance, and Frank Gehry's American Center. This houses the famous Cinémathèque Française, a wonderful cinema museum that hosts frequent retrospectives of famous directors.

At the foot of these structures, the imaginatively designed 14-ha (35-acre) Parc de Bercy provides a welcome green space for this part of the city.

Former wine stores and cellars along Cours St-Émilion have been restored as bars, restaurants and shops, and one of the warehouses now contains the Musée des Arts Forains (Fairground Museum), open for private tours only.

Merci
📍 M6 🏛 111 Boulevard Beaumarchais 75003
Ⓜ St-Sébastien Froissart
🕐 10:30am-7:30pm Mon-Thu (to 8pm Fri & Sat), 11am-7:30pm Sun
🌐 merci-merci.com

Paris has grand department stores and luxury boutiques aplenty, but around Bastille, Merci is the place for retail therapy. A small concept store housed in an old wall-paper factory, it opened in 2009 and curates the best in fashion and design. Homewares, clothes, accessories and kitchen products are housed under a glass atrium, spread across multiple floors.

It has none of the glitz or brand names of big-brother department stores like Printemps or Le Bon Marché. Instead, it reflects

Did You Know?

Paris's 11th arrondissement is one of the most densely populated districts in Europe.

the neighbourhood's character, featuring many independent designers and local brands. If you're not interested in swiping your cards on trendy accessories, you could join the locals at Merci's popular restaurant and two cafés. The Used Book Café, set among towering shelves of literature, is especially appealing for afternoon tea or coffee. Fresh salads, egg dishes and *tartines* are all on the menu.

The shop also houses temporary exhibitions and pop-up events that manage to keep it feeling fresh and exciting.

Cour Damoye and Passage du Cheval Blanc

📍N7 Ⓜ Bastille, Voltaire, Bréguet Sabin

Amid the bustle of Place de la Bastille, there are tiny enclaves of calm hidden in two historic passages, the Cour Damoye and the Passage du Cheval

Blanc. Most people walk right by their entrances without daring to enter, but these walkways are open to the public.

This area has been a centre of carpentry and French furniture design since the time of the Middle Ages. Its location near a port on the Seine that dealt with wood and timber made it popular with craftspeople, and many high-end artisans producing fine furnishings can still be found in the district.

The late-18th-century Cour Damoye is today largely residential, with a few small businesses still functioning, but remnants of its former artisan workshops are visible in the façades. The Passage du Cheval Blanc, just off Rue de la Roquette, is named after the sign of a horse that once adorned the entrance. Offering a peaceful respite from the busy Faubourg

FURNITURE-MAKING DISTRICT

Close to the former docks at Quai de la Rapée, the Faubourg St-Antoine district east of the Place de la Bastille served to stock lumber, leading to its renown as a centre for furniture- and cabinet-making and their related trades. The craftsmanship even caught the eye of Louis XIV, and his Minister of Finances, Colbert, established the royal mirror factory here. Today, there are still antique sellers and craftspeople dotted around Rue du Faubourg St-Antoine, especially on Le Passage du Chantier.

St-Antoine, its small labyrinth of cobbled courtyards, named after the months of the year (Cour de Janvier etc), hide architecture companies and apartments, with wooden beams still visible in some buildings. The Cité Parchappe spills you back out onto the main road.

←

The former wine-trading district of Bercy, and *(inset)* Parc de Bercy

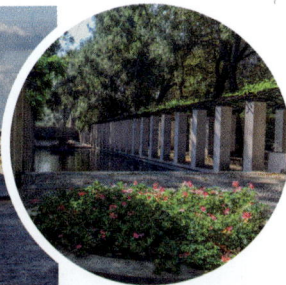

RÉPUBLIQUE AND CANAL ST-MARTIN

These areas have recently transformed into exciting, somewhat quirky destinations. Characterized by the *bobos* (bohemian-bourgeois Parisians) who helped remodel it, the canal is a hotspot for daytime coffee dates and evening picnics, fuelled by an extensive selection of cafés. Shoppers should head to the pockets of boutiques specializing in homeware, clothing and jewellery. This is the side of Paris that few visitors see but are exceedingly happy to find.

Patrons at a café in the
neighbourhood around
Canal St-Martin

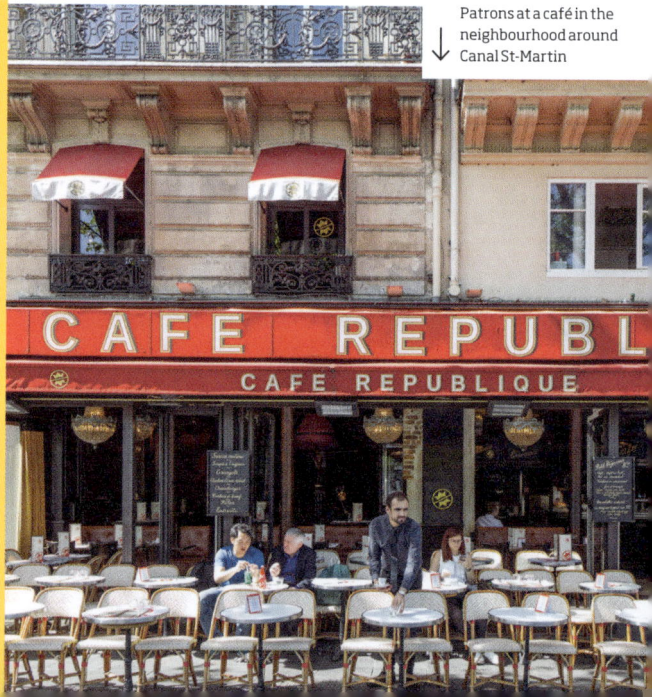

← Picturesque Canal St-Martin

CANAL ST-MARTIN

📍 M4 Ⓜ Jacques Bonsergent, Goncourt, République
🚌 26, 46, 75

...ating back to the time of Napoleon, this 4.5-km (2.5-mile) waterway flows through one of Paris's ...rendiest districts. Colourful shops and cafés ...ne its banks, where locals spend weekends ...icnicking or cycling along the waterfront.

...tretching between the Seine in the south and the ...assin de la Villette in the north, the Canal St-Martin ...pened in 1825 as a means of bringing fresh water ...o Paris's polluted city centre. However, in the late ...9th century part of the canal was covered to make ...ay for new roadways, and within a few decades the ...anal and the boats that worked upon it had become ...bsolete. City officials almost drained and filled ...ne entire waterway in the 1970s, but by the turn ...f the millennium it had become a popular location ...r wealthy young Parisians to buy and renovate ...roperties. This once-derelict district is now one of ...ne Right Bank's most desirable areas, a culturally ...ixed neighbourhood where Paris's hipsters mingle ...mong families and international arrivals.

DRINK

Here are the best coffee shops around the canal:

Ten Belles
📍 M4 🏠 10 Rue de la Grange aux Belles 75010 🌐 tenbelles.com

Holybelly
📍 L4 🏠 5 & 19 Rue Lucien Sampaix 75010 🌐 holy bellycafe.com

Caoua Coffee Stop
📍 M4 🏠 98 Quai de Jemmapes 75010 📞 09 50 73 47 17

EXPERIENCE MORE

Square du Temple

📍 L5 📫 75003
Ⓜ Temple, République

A quiet and pleasant park today, this was once a fortified centre of the medieval Knights Templar. A state within a state, the area contained a palace, a church and shops behind high walls and a draw-bridge, making it a haven for those who were seeking to escape from royal jurisdiction. Louis XVI and Marie-Antoinette were held in the Temple fortress after their arrest in 1792. The king set out from here for his execution by guillotine.

Gare du Nord

📍 L2 📫 18 Rue de Dunkerque 75010
Ⓜ Gare du Nord

Opened in 1864, this train station is best known today as the hub for the Eurostar to London, as well as services to Brussels and Amsterdam. This massive station is Europe's busiest, with over 200 million passengers per year. The imposing façade is dotted with sculptures representing other European capitals, including Berlin and London. The soaring iron structure inside creates a romantic departure hall, and has been used as a film location for several movies. Inside the station, a new wave of cafés and restaurants is reinventing the travelling experience, as well as the surrounding neighbourhood. The station has undergone further refurbishments for the 2024 Olympic Games.

Hôpital St-Louis

📍 M4 📫 1 Ave Claude Vellefaux 75010
Ⓜ Goncourt, Colonel Fabien

Built by order of King Henri IV in 1607 and completed after his death, this hospital originally served the growing number of plague victims at the time. Patients crowded into the rooms surrounding the square courtyard, reminiscent of Place des Vosges in the Marais, and constructed by the same architect.

Did You Know?

The Square du Temple contains 70 species of trees, including an 18-m- (59-ft-) tall Turkish hazel.

SHOP

Marché des Enfants Rouges

This market, founded in 1628, on Rue de Bretagne is full of food stalls and international cuisine, and is usually packed at lunchtime.

📍 M6 📫 39 Rue de Bretagne 75003
🕐 Mon

Most would never see the sky again except for a rare stroll through that grassy courtyard. Conditions in the hospital worsened over time, but eventually the plague passed. The building later served as a dermatology hospital and a prison for nuns during the French Revolution.

Today, modern facilities next to the 17th-century buildings still function as a hospital. A small adjacent chapel – built for local farmers and not for plague victims – was used for King Henri IV's funeral in 1610. The main courtyard is open to the public and is an almost hauntingly calm respite in the heart of Paris. One of its wings is home to the Musée des Moulages, an informative museum dedicated to skin diseases.

Musée des Moulages

📍M4 🏠1 Ave Claude Vellefaux 75010 📞01 42 49 86 Ⓜ Goncourt, Colonel Fabien 🕐9am–4:30pm Mon–Fri; advance bookings required, call ahead

Housed inside the Hôpital St-Louis, this museum has 4,807 wax moulds of horrific skin diseases of the 1800s. Dr Lallier of the Hôpital St-Louis hired Jules Baretta, a wax-fruit maker, to create models of real diseases to teach students about things such as syphilis and elephantiasis. Baretta would spend time with patients in the hospital, carefully using plaster of Paris to create his moulds. He would then paint them in great detail, even adding hair to keep them realistic. While many of the faces and body parts are unsettling in their realism, they are true works of art. Cyclopoid babies, various stages of then-fatal syphilis, and all sorts of abnormal skin growths are as fascinating as they are gruesome. The collection is an enlightening look into

how far medicine has come in the past 150 years, to a time before the discovery of antibiotics that could cure many of these diseases.

Today, few students visit the antiquated learning tools, so the museum is often empty. Call ahead to arrange an appointment, and purchase tickets within the modern hospital's reception, adjacent to the original structure. Children under 12 are not allowed.

Musée des Arts et Métiers

📍L5 🏠60 Rue Réaumur 75003 Ⓜ Arts et Métiers 🕐10am–6pm Tue–Sun (to 9pm Thu) 🚫1 Jan, 1 May, 25 Dec 🌐arts-et-metiers.net

Housed within the old Abbey of St-Martin-des-Champs, the Arts and Crafts Museum was founded in 1794. After major renovations in the 1990s it reopened in 2000 as an excellent museum of science and industry displaying 5,000 items (it has 75,000 additional artifacts in storage that are available to academics and researchers). The museum explores the theme of man's ingenuity and the worlds of invention and manufacturing, covering such topics as textiles, photography and machines. Among the most entertaining displays are those of musical clocks, mechanical musical instruments and automata (mechanical figures). One of these figures, the "Joueuse de Tympanon", is said to represent Marie-Antoinette.

→

A plane on display at the Musée des Arts et Métiers

Gare de l'Est

◉ L3 ⌂ Place du 11 Novembre 1918 75010 Ⓜ Gare de l'Est

Whether travelling to Germany or just passing through the neighbourhood, visitors should take a moment to marvel at one of Paris's oldest train stations. Opened in 1849, it had doubled in size by 1931 after several renovations. Statues atop the façade represent Strasbourg and Verdun, two of the original destinations served by the station. In 1883, the very first *Orient Express* departed from Gare de l'Est for Istanbul. Inside the main hall, a massive painting by American artist Albert Herter depicts French troops leaving the station for the Front during World War I in 1914. German forces transformed an underground air-raid shelter into a wartime bunker during World War II, which is still preserved under the station, though it is not open to visitors.

Rue Ste-Marthe

◉ N4 ⌂ 75010 Ⓜ Goncourt, Belleville

Just north of the Hôpital St-Louis, this little street feels more like a walk through some southern provincial French town than central Paris. Colourful doors and façades contrast with the often grey Parisian skies. Each one opens up to an artist's studio, a workshop, a quirky restaurant, or some oddball boutique. There is little historical significance in these former workers' quarters, but the area is a unique slice of Parisian life. Look for olives in the

---

🔍 HIDDEN GEM
Marché St-Quentin

The 19th-century covered market Marché St-Quentin on Boulevard de Magenta makes a handy stop for last-minute cheese and wine before you board a train from the Gare de l'Est or Gare du Nord.

The impressive interior of Gare de l'Est

independent grocery, try some Vietnamese food, or spend an evening with a glass of wine and charcuterie at any of the local bars here. Tourists rarely make it this far, stopping instead at the Canal St-Martin. A walk along Rue Sainte-Marthe, however, is a very Parisian experience.

Portes St-Denis et St-Martin

📍 K4, L4 🏠 Blvds St-Denis & St-Martin 75010 Ⓜ Strasbourg-St-Denis

These imposing gates give access to the two ancient and important thoroughfares whose names they bear, running across Paris in a north–south direction.

They once marked the entrance to the city. The impressive Porte St-Denis is 23 m (76 ft) high and was built in 1672 by François Blondel. It is decorated with figures by Louis XIV's sculptor, François Girardon and commemorates the victories of the king's armies in Flanders and the Rhine that year. Porte St-Martin is 17 m (56 ft) tall and was built in 1674 by Pierre Bullet, a student of Blondel. It celebrates the capture of Besançon and the defeat of the Triple Alliance of Spain, Holland and Germany.

EAT & DRINK

Le Plomb du Cantal

A local establishment serving well-prepared, no-frills, traditional French food.

📍 L4 🏠 4 Bvld St-Denis 75010 Ⓦ leplombdu cantal.com

€€€

SAam

Korean street food pairs with rice wine, sake and daily juices at this hip, fun restaurant.

📍 M4 🏠 59 bis Rue de Lancry 75010 📞 09 83 50 84 94

€€€

Le Comptoir Général

This quirky venue hosts events and has a bar popular during the evenings and on Sunday afternoons.

📍 M4 🏠 80 Quai de Jemmapes 75010 Ⓦ lecomptoir general.com

La Barav

This popular wine bar fills up with locals sharing bottles and cheese plates.

📍 M5 🏠 6 Rue Charles-François Dupuis 75003 Ⓦ lebarav.fr

Le Mary Celeste

Go for cocktails, stay for the small plates, and then have more cocktails.

📍 M6 🏠 1 Rue Commines 75003 Ⓦ lemaryceleste.com

BELLEVILLE AND MÉNILMONTANT

Far from the beaten path, Belleville and Ménilmontant are local enclaves that are little visited by tourists. Artists toil away in their galleries and in the streets, turning thoroughfares such as Rue Dénoyez into open-air artworks, while Asian restaurants and shops attract locals who want a break from duck *confit*. Hipsters and international residents have made their home in these characterful areas, which offer a rewarding glimpse into everyday Parisian life.

One of the many street art murals in Belleville
↓

↑ A visitor strolling along a leafy lane at the fascinating Cimetière du Père Lachaise

Must See

MUR DES FÉDÉRÉS

Following France's defeat in the Franco-Prussian War in 1871, a left-wing group revolted, setting up the Paris Commune. After 72 days, government troops marched on the city and in a week of brutal street fighting, much of the city was burned and thousands were killed. Mur des Fédérés (The Communards' Wall) in Père Lachaise is where the last Communard rebels were executed by government forces.

CIMETIÈRE DU PÈRE LACHAISE

📍 R6 🏠 Blvd de Ménilmontant 75020 Ⓜ Père Lachaise, Alexandre Dumas 🚌 26, 60, 61, 64, 69 to Pl Gambetta 🕐 8am–5:30pm Mon–Fri, 8:30am–5:30pm Sat, 9am–5:30pm Sun (mid-Mar–Oct: to 6pm daily)

This is the most visited cemetery in the world. It contains over 70,000 graves, including the tombs of numerous famous figures, such as the writer Honoré de Balzac, the composer Frédéric Chopin, the singer Jim Morrison and the actor Yves Montand.

Paris's most prestigious cemetery is set on a wooded hill overlooking the city. The land was once owned by Père de la Chaise, Louis XIV's confessor, but it was bought in 1803 by order of Napoleon to create a new cemetery. Père Lachaise, the first cemetery in France with a crematorium, became so popular that it was expanded six times during the 19th century.

Today, the cemetery is a place of pilgrimage for rock fans, who come from around the world to see the grave of Jim Morrison of The Doors. With its moss-grown tombs and ancient trees, as well as striking funerary sculpture, Père Lachaise is an atmospheric and rather romantic place for a stroll.

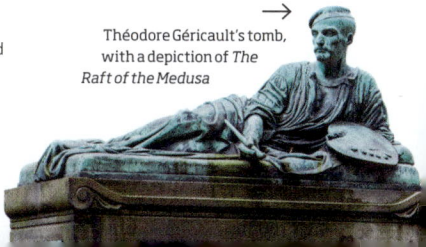

→ Théodore Géricault's tomb, with a depiction of *The Raft of the Medusa*

EXPERIENCE MORE

Parc de Belleville

📍 Q4 🏠 47 Rue des Couronnes 75020 Ⓜ Couronnes, Belleville 🕐 Oct–May: 8am–dusk daily; Jun–Sep: 7am–dusk daily

It has less of the manicured appeal of some of Paris's other parks, but the Parc de Belleville has views that no other green space can offer. This steep garden offers unparalleled panoramas of Paris, including the Eiffel Tower and Notre-Dame. The hill was originally settled by religious orders, who purchased parcels of land and planted vines. *Guinguettes* popped up in the Middle Ages, the outdoor pubs or beer gardens of their day. It was here that Parisians drank "*piquette*", a young wine from the area, which today is also French slang for bad wine. Eventually windmills dominated the landscape, owing to the park's altitude.

The park is a welcome green space in densely populated east Paris. Between the patches of exquisitely maintained flowerbeds are stairs and pathways criss-crossed by waterways and trestles. There is even a waterfall that trickles 100 m (328 ft) from the top of the grounds to the bottom. In a throwback to Belleville's winemaking past, 140 grapevines grow on the slopes, and the grapes are harvested each year.

Rue de Belleville

📍 P4 🏠 75020 Ⓜ Belleville, Pyrénées, Jourdain

The main street of the former Belleville village, Rue de Belleville cuts through the district from Belleville Metro station. The street used to be the location of the old wall that separated Paris from its suburbs. Belleville gets its name from a deformation of the French words *belle vue*, or "beautiful view" – the reason for which becomes apparent when you look downhill from the street towards where the Eiffel Tower rises up in the distance. The stretch between the Metro stations Belleville and Pyrénées is the most interesting. At No 72, a plaque commemorates the birth in 1915 of Edith Piaf, who, according to popular legend, was born here on the steps. Over the past decades, many multicultural restaurants and East Asian shops have sprung up along the street as immigrants have moved into the area, and all sorts of exciting and inexpensive food items can be found here. Restaurants such as Ama Siam, at No 49, serving traditional homemade Laotian and Thai dishes, and Chez René et Gabin, at 92 Boulevard Belleville, specializing in Tunisian cuisine, make it worth the hike up the hilly street.

La Bellevilloise

📍 Q5 🏠 19 Rue Boyer 75020 Ⓜ Ménilmontant, Gambetta 🌐 labelle villoise.com

Set up in 1877, this community art centre's original aim was to bring cultural education to less affluent Parisians. This spirit lives on in its numerous events, which include

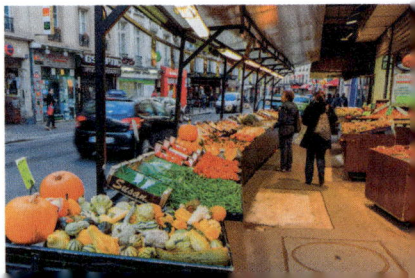

concerts – often jazz or Latin – and art exhibits, as well as freelancer fairs, vintage markets and the occasional jazz brunch. A standout feature is the Halle aux Olives, a glass atrium performance area with tables surrounded by an urban jungle of sorts.

Rue Dénoyez
Q P4 **A** 75020
M Belleville

Throughout Paris, street artists take advantage of any surface they can. In Rue Dénoyez, however, it seems as if the city actively encourages it. This narrow street, tucked away off Rue de Belleville and formerly rather run down, is essentially an outdoor contemporary art gallery where street artists constantly leave their mark. It is named after a local family who ran a popular dance hall in the 1830s, but today it is all about street art, reflecting the lively, bohemian spirit of the neighbourhood. On any given day, someone will be out there, spray-painting their newest mural on one of the walls. The buildings are mostly artists' studios – some will let you in if you are lucky – but the

←

real draw is the colourful and daring works on the walls. In recent years, some of the studios have been replaced by more modern social housing, but the artistic spirit of Rue Dénoyez remains. Parisians still gather at the end of the street at Aux Folies, a bar known for its cheap drinks and a sea of plastic chairs spilling onto the pavement, while at the other end of the street Le Barbouquin is a great place to relax with a drink and a book from one of its groaning shelves.

Quartier Jourdain
Q Q3 **A** 75020
M Jourdain

If you are looking to get away from the crowds but still get a taste of Parisian life, an afternoon wandering the Jourdain quarter is a perfect start. Sprawling out from the Neo-Gothic St-Jean-Baptiste church, the area has slowly come into its own. The central square, full of cafés and quintessentially Parisian shops – cheese here, meat there, pastries everywhere – is little visited by tourists; this is one of the rare districts of Paris that still retains a village feel. It might be towards the edge of the city, but it is a quick and easy trip on Line 11 of the Metro from Hôtel de Ville in the centre. The nearby Parc des Buttes-

Chaumont pairs nicely with a visit to Jourdain, as does a detour to Le Plateau on Rue des Alouettes, an industrial-white exhibition space run by Frac (the Fonds Régional D'Art Contemporain, or regional collection of contemporary art). It displays modern art – including paintings, photography and everything in between – from its 1,600-piece collection. There's also occasional performance art.

DRINK

Aux Folies
Plastic chairs all over the terrace give this a homey feel, reinforced by cheap drinks and loud locals.

Q P4 **A** 8 Rue de Belleville 75020
C 06 28 55 89 40

Le Barbouquin
This cosy café - part coffee shop, part bar and part book-shop/library - is an ideal chill-out spot. It hosts regular music nights.

Q P4 **A** 1 Rue Dénoyez 75020
C 09 84 32 13 21

EAT

Ravioli Nord-Est

It's all about the dumplings here – cheap and delicious.

📍N4 🏠11 Rue Civiale 75010
📞01 75 50 88 03
🕐Wed

€ €€

La Baratin

An institution; go to experience quintessentially meaty French fare.

📍Q4 🏠3 Rue Jouye-Rouve 75020
📞01 43 49 39 70
🕐Sun, Tue

€€€

Marché de Belleville

📍P4 🏠Blvd de Belleville 75020 Ⓜ Belleville
🕐7am–2:30pm Tue & Fri

Every Tuesday and Friday morning, the Belleville outdoor market comes alive, stretching from the Belleville Metro station to Couronnes. It dates back to the 19th century, when it was just a little market for the independent commune outside Paris's wall, and is still a popular and inexpensive source of fresh produce for eastern Parisians. The stalls follow the seasons, with juicy clementines in the winter, strawberries in the spring, and the best tomatoes in late summer. Some stalls sell odds and ends such as wine openers, French candy bars and bags of olives – it's the place to stock up on anything and everything. Vendors yell out prices, pushing the foods that need to go. By the end of the market, they start selling large piles of produce for a euro, so there are true bargains to be had. The locals pile into the crowded market rain or shine, so be prepared to manoeuvre around Parisians arguing about bruised apples.

Église St-Jean-Baptiste

📍Q3 🏠139 Rue de Belleville 75019
Ⓜ Jourdain 🕐9:30am–8:30pm Mon, 8:15am–7:45pm Tue–Sun (to 8:30pm Fri) 🌐sjbb.fr

As far as churches go, the Neo-Gothic St-Jean-Baptiste de Belleville flies under the radar of most people in Paris. Set high above the city in a vibrant district full of shops, it's an exciting find for architecture enthusiasts. Built to replace the original church dating back to the 1600s, the current structure was erected between 1854 and 1859. The architect, Jean-Baptiste Antoine Lassus, was a specialist in medieval architecture. He is largely responsible for bringing back Gothic themes in modern structures and participated heavily in the restorations of Notre-Dame and other monuments. Though a master in his craft, Lassus is often overlooked for the more famous Viollet-le-Duc, who lauded this structure after Lassus' death. It was, in fact, Lassus' final project. This church, with its twin bell towers and vaulted ceilings, evokes the grandeur of churches such as the Sainte-Chapelle.

La Campagne à Paris

📍Q6 🏠Rue du Père-Prosper-Enfantin, Rue Mondonville, Rue Irénée Blanc, Rue Jules Siegfried 75020
Ⓜ Porte de Bagnolet

This former housing estate is one of the most picturesque parts of Paris, with stone-fronted houses lining the cobbled streets. La Campagne, literally "the countryside", feels exactly like that. A pastor, Sully Lombard, conceived of the development in 1907 for lower-income Parisians.

Built on the site of an old gypsum quarry and completed well after World War I, the 90-odd houses stood out from the rest of Paris's architecture. Brick façades, creeping ivy and wisteria, and tiny gated gardens full of roses and clematis adorn the two-storey houses. These provincial-looking cobbled streets offer some splendid photo opportunities and are a wonderful oasis of calm away from the bustle of urban Paris.

La Maroquinerie

📍 Q5 🏠 23 Rue Boyer 75020 Ⓜ Ménilmontant, Gambetta 🌐 lamaroquinerie.fr

True music fans will want to visit this former leather workshop turned concert venue. It's intimate, with a capacity of about 500, and has hosted some big names before they hit success. Bruno Mars and Sam Fender are just some of the acts who have played here. The bohemian-chic venue also has a restaurant with a constantly changing menu of French classics, and a terrace bar for drinking the night away. Book in advance for a wide range of musical productions.

Notre-Dame-de-la-Croix

📍 Q5 🏠 3 Place de Ménilmontant 75020 Ⓜ Ménilmontant, Couronnes 🕐 8am-7:30pm Tue-Sun (to 7pm Sun) 🌐 notredamedelacroix.com

Consecrated in 1863 under the reign of Napoleon III, this stunning church looms over Ménilmontant, built as the population of the area boomed. Its architecture is an odd mix of Romanesque and Gothic elements, with an enormous tower reaching 78 m (256 ft) high. In terms of size, it's actually the third-largest church in Paris after Notre-Dame and St-Sulpice. This district was particularly caught up by the Paris Commune of 1871, when Parisians rose up against the government, which had been exiled to Versailles by Prussian forces. During this turbulent time the Communards, as the rebels were known, held meetings in Notre-Dame-de-la-Croix. It was here that they made the decision to execute the Archbishop, Georges Darboy, who had been taken hostage by the Communards on 24 May at the prison on Rue de la Roquette.

The church does not stir up much of this stormy history, but instead offers a splendid visit devoid of the tourists crushed into other monuments. Look out for the organ, constructed in two separate parts to avoid obstructing the rose window overhead. The church also has two major artworks: *Christ in Limbo* (1819) by Pierre Delorme and *Christ Curing the Sick* (1827) by Jean-Pierre Granger.

→

The Neo-Romanesque façade of Notre-Dame-de-la-Croix

LA VILLETTE

On the city's northeast edge, the canal cuts a broad path through this green park that's as family friendly as it is cultural. The stunning Jean Nouvel-designed Philharmonie towers look like a spaceship while the science centre and playground across the water provide endless entertainment for kids. Joggers and cyclists appreciate the traffic-free pathways, and in spring and summer concerts and outdoor movies soundtrack the evenings. Parisians of all ages head here to while away the time with a glass of rosé as the clinking of their *pétanque* balls echoes over the water.

↓ The Philharmonie de Paris, designed by Jean Nouvel

OPEN-AIR FILM FESTIVAL

Each summer the park hosts the free Cinéma en Plein Air festival, screening a mix of French and international films in the open air several evenings a week for a month. Deckchairs and blankets are available for hire, and many people bring their own picnic to make an evening of it.

↑ Taking time out in the sunshine in front of one of the cafés in the park

PARC DE LA VILLETTE

📍 Q1 🏠 211 Ave Jean Jaurès 75019 Ⓜ Porte de Pantin, Porte de la Villette 🚌 75, 139, 150, 151, 152 🚊 T3b 🕐 Hours vary, check website Ⓦ lavillette.com

This inventive urban park offers an appealing combination of nature and modern architecture, containing gardens, playgrounds and a variety of cultural spaces.

26

The number of jaunty, red, modern follies that brighten up the park.

Urban Regeneration

Once home to slaughterhouses and a livestock market, this former industrial area has been transformed into a vibrant urban park. Designed by Bernard Tschumi, its vast facilities cover 55 ha (136 acres) of a previously run-down part of the city. The plan was to revive the tradition of parks for meetings and activities, and to stimulate interest in the arts and sciences. Work began in 1984, and the park has grown to include the Cité des Sciences et de l'Industrie – a high-tech hands-on science museum – a cutting-edge concert hall, an exhibition pavilion, a spherical cinema, a circus and a major live-music venue (Le Zénith) and a jazz club (La Petite Villette). Linking them all is the park itself, Paris's third largest, with its follies, walkways, gardens and playgrounds, one of the most popular being the Jardin du Dragon with its huge long slide. In the summer, the park holds several festivals, including an open-air film event and jazz festival.

Must See

↑ The Story of the Universe, taking visitors back 13.7 billion years to the creation of the first atom

Le grand récit de l'Univers

CITÉ DES SCIENCES ET DE L'INDUSTRIE

Q1 🏠 30 Ave Corentin Cariou 75019 Ⓜ Porte de la Villette 🚍 75, 139, 150, 152 🚋 T3b 🕙 10am–6pm Tue–Sat (to 7pm Sun); advance booking recommended, check website 🚫 1 Jan, 1 May, 25 Dec 🌐 cite-sciences.fr

Located within the Parc de la Villette, the Cité des Sciences et de l'Industrie is an interactive science and technology museum that is hugely popular with families.

The museum occupies the largest of the old Villette slaughterhouses. Architect Adrien Fainsilber has created an imaginative interplay of light, vegetation and water in the high-tech, five-storey building, which soars 40 m (133 ft) high, stretching over 3 ha (7 acres). At the museum's heart are permanent exhibitions on themes including space exploration, climate change, genetics and sound; the exhibits are further augmented by interactive, computerized games. On other levels, there is a planetarium and the Cité des Enfants (book ahead for a 90-minute slot) where children can learn about scientific phenomena through fun experiments.

LA GÉODE

Fittingly for a building that looks as if its from the set of a sci-fi movie, this Adrien Fainsilber-designed sphere houses a vast cinema showing IMAX and 3D films, as well as a futuristic outdoor playground. The Géode is closed for refurbishment, but is well worth admiring from the outside.

EXPERIENCE MORE

Parc des Buttes-Chaumont

Q2 **A** Rue Botzaris 75019 (main access from Rue Armand Carrel) **M** Botzaris, Buttes-Chaumont **O** 7am-9pm daily (May-Aug: to 10pm; Oct-Mar: to 8pm)

For many, this is the most pleasant and unexpected park in the city. The panoramic hilly site was formerly a gallows for the execution of criminals, a lime quarry and a rubbish dump. It was converted in the mid-1860s, one of Napoleon III's many projects to renovate the city. Baron Haussmann worked with the landscape architect and designer Adolphe Alphand, who organized a vast programme to furnish the new pavement-lined avenues with benches and lampposts.

Others involved in the creation of this large park were the engineer Darcel and the landscape gardener Barillet-Deschamps. They created a lake, made an island with real and artificial rocks, gave it a Roman-style classical temple (the Temple de la Sibylle, modelled after the Temple of Sybil in Tivoli, Italy). The pair also added a waterfall, streams, and two footbridges to connect the island to the park.

MK2 Quai de Loire and Quai de Seine

N2 **A** 7 Quai de la Loire, 14 Quai de la Seine 75019 **M** Stalingrad, Jaurès **W** mk2.com

These two cinemas on opposite banks of the canal basin are popular hangouts during the evenings. Neighbouring cafés and bars fill with cinephiles who are waiting to see the latest release. The cinemas screen a large selection of French and international movies that cater to both art-house and blockbuster crowds, sometimes showing Hollywood pictures before their US release.

When buying a ticket, note which cinema your film is in; if it's on the opposite bank, a water shuttle will carry you across the canal. Bear in mind that international films are shown in VO *(version originale)* or VF *(version française)*. If you don't want to watch a film dubbed into French buy tickets for the VO version. Afterwards, you could join a game of *pétanque* along the canal, just next to the cinema, where Parisians while away their evenings.

EAT

La Rotonde

Part of Paris's last great peripherary wall, this Classical-style rotonda is now a great stop for a meal or cocktails.

N2 **A** 6-8 Place de la Bataille de Stalingrad 75019 **W** larotonde stalingrad.com

€€€

---

25 Degrés Est

With a terrace overlooking the canal, this laid-back bar-restaurant attracts sun-seekers in the summer.

N2 **A** 10 Place de la Bataille de Stalingrad 75019 **C** 09 53 27 68 16

€€€

Simonetta

Enjoy excellent Neapolitan-style pizzas on the bustling canalside terrace of this restaurant.

Q1 **A** 32 Quai de la Marne 75019 **W** sim onetta-paris.com

€€€

#104

📍N1 🏠5 Rue Curial
75019 Ⓜ Stalingrad,
Riquet 🕐Noon-7pm
Tue-Sun, 11am-7pm
Sat & Sun 🌐104.fr

It might not be obvious upon entering, but this art centre was originally built by the Parisian Archbishop in 1874 for funeral services. It housed a coffin warehouse, stables for horses and shops where individuals could purchase decorations for tombs. Eventually the hearses of the 20th century disappeared when the public sector lost its monopoly on conducting funeral services.

The space, however, underwent a renaissance. The vast hall, with iron beams and a glass roof, was slowly transformed into # 104 (or Centquatre-Paris), an artists' residence and exhibition space. The centre is an excellent example of urban renewal in a city skilled at repurposing its historic structures. The mayor inaugurated the space in 2008, and the city still funds the majority of its costs. Today there are performances, concerts and art shows year-round,

open to the public. Visitors can see artists at work experimenting with different media.

Centquatre-Paris is quickly becoming a major player on the art scene among local and international artists: it has hosted exhibitions dedicated to well-known contemporary artists such as Keith Haring and Krijn de Koning.

Philharmonie de Paris

📍R1 🏠221 Ave Jean Jaurès 75019 Ⓜ Porte de Pantin 🕐Museum: noon-6pm Tue-Fri, 10am-6pm Sat & Sun 🌐philhar moniedeparis.fr

Built in 2015, the futuristic Philharmonie, designed by French architect Jean Nouvel, rises above Parc de la Villette like a silver spaceship. Visitors can ascend to the rooftop in free lifts at the entrance and enjoy wonderful views

over Paris (and get a bite to eat at the panoramic restaurant) before walking back down to ground level via the "Chemin de Montagne" walkway that snakes around the building. Inside, the main concert hall seats up to 3,650 people, depending on the configuration and the placement of floating balconies. The idea is that spectators are never further than 32 m (105 ft) from the conductor, creating a more immersive, intimate experience.

The Philharmonie caters mostly to symphonic concerts, but also hosts jazz and world music performances. It houses cultural centres and exhibition halls, as well as smaller concert halls. Smaller scale concerts are also held at the neighbouring Cité de la Musique, now rechristened Philharmonie 2, where the Musée de la Musique

→
The rooftop of
Jean Nouvel's
Philharmonie de Paris

also housed. Here, more than 1,000 instruments – including Chopin's piano and Georges Brassens' guitar – illustrate the development of Western music from the 17th century. Audio guides provide excellent excerpts of music, too.

La Grande Halle de la Villette

📍 Q1 🏠 211 Ave Jean Jaurès 75019
Ⓜ Porte de Pantin
🌐 lavillette.com

A former slaughterhouse, this huge hall is one of three that were once in this part of La Villette. In the 19th century, Haussmann decided it would be easier to concentrate all of the meat industry in one spot. Eventually, and perhaps unsurprisingly, the area gained the nickname "City of Blood".

In the 1980s, the veal hall was destroyed while the sheep hall was reconstructed in hopes of rebuilding it elsewhere. President Mitterrand preserved this iron beauty, once used for slaughtering cows for beef, and today it houses an event space. Concerts, plays, exhibitions and other events take place here regularly. You can also drop into the café plus restaurant at the complex for a coffee or meal; it has

an inviting garden area for when the weather is fair.

Cabaret Sauvage

📍 Q1 🏠 59 Blvd Macdonald 75019
Ⓜ Porte de la Villette
🌐 cabaretsauvage.com

On the bank of the canal, just before it leaves Paris's city limits, a curious venue stands by itself in the Parc de la Villette. Opened in 1997, the Cabaret Sauvage is an entertainment venue unlike any other in Paris. Algerian-born Méziane Azaïche created the space, which welcomes all sorts of up-and-coming and little-known artists. Concerts and shows range from contemporary acrobatic and circus displays to dance and West African musical performances, and international artists such as Redman, Mos Def and Noel Gallagher have played here over the years.

Inside the red velour draping, spectators cannot help but be drawn into the Cabaret Sauvage's unique circus-ring atmosphere: there are bevelled mirrors, banquettes and a circular dance floor. Renovations have resulted in improved acoustics, plus a wide terrace for open-air events. A night out at the Cabaret Sauvage is sure to be as memorable as it is individual.

DRINK

Point Éphémère
Part concert hall, part drinking venue. There are often special nights with food trucks or other pop-ups.

📍 N2 🏠 200 Quai de Valmy 75010
🌐 pointephemere.org

Paname Brewing Company
Perched on the canal in an old warehouse; local craft beers are the favourite here.

📍 P1 🏠 41 bis Quai de la Loire 75019
🌐 panamebrewing company.com

Le Pavillon Puebla
Nestled in the greenery of Parc des Buttes-Chaumont, this is a peaceful oasis with a mix of Moroccan and modern touches.

📍 P3 🏠 Ave Darcel 75019 🌐 leper choir.fr

MONTMARTRE AND PIGALLE

Although the area around the Moulin Rouge is still dotted with sordid "love" shops and seedy bars, Montmartre and Pigalle have become fashionable destinations for diners and shoppers. Pigalle's red lights have given way to some of the city's best pastry shops, boutique hotels and designer stores. Visitors still love browsing the art at Place du Tertre and soaking up the view of Paris from atop hilly Montmartre, where the cobbled streets and quaint houses retain a 19th-century village feel that few other districts reproduce.

The stunning view from the Sacré-Coeur in Montmartre

↓

SACRÉ-COEUR

📍 J1 🏠 33 Rue du Chevalier-de-la-Barre 75018 Ⓜ Abbesses (then take funicular to the steps of the Sacré-Coeur), Anvers, Barbès-Rochechouart, Lamarck-Caulaincourt 🚌 30, 31, 40, 80, 85 🕐 6:30am-10:30pm daily; dome: 10:30am-5pm daily (Mar-May: to 7pm; Jun-Sep: to 8:30pm) 🅦 sacre-coeur-montmartre.com

Situated atop the hill of Montmartre, the spectacular white basilica of the Sacré-Coeur watches over Paris from the city's highest point. It stands as a memorial to the 58,000 French soldiers killed during the Franco-Prussian War.

Six months after the outbreak of the Franco-Prussian War in 1870, two Catholic businessmen made a private religious vow to build a church dedicated to the Sacred Heart of Christ as penance for France's sins. The two men, Alexandre Legentil and Hubert Rohault de Fleury, vowed to see Paris saved from invasion despite the war and a lengthy siege – and were able to witness the start of work on the Sacré-Coeur basilica. The project was taken up by Archbishop Guibert of Paris and construction began in 1875 to Paul Abadie's designs, which were inspired by the Romano-Byzantine church of St-Front in Périgueux. The basilica was completed in 1914, but its consecration was forestalled by World War I until 1919, after France was victorious.

THE SIEGE OF PARIS

Prussia invaded France in 1870. During this gruelling four-month siege of Paris, instigated by the Prusso-German statesman Otto von Bismarck, hungry Parisians were forced to eat the city's horses and other animals.

📷 PICTURE PERFECT
The Basilica and the City

The best view of the Sacré-Coeur is from the gardens below, but for a 360-degree panorama of the city, climb the 300 steps to the top of the basilica dome.

→ The beautiful basilica, crowned by its elegant ovoid dome

EXPERIENCE MORE

St-Pierre de Montmartre

📍 J1 🏠 2 Rue du Mont-Cenis 75018 Ⓜ Abbesses ⏰ 8am–7pm daily (to 6pm Fri) ✉ saintpierredemontmartre.net

Situated in the shadow of the Sacré-Coeur basilica, St-Pierre de Montmartre is all that remains of the great Benedictine Abbey of Montmartre, which was founded in 1133 by Louis VI and his wife, Adelaide of Savoy, who – as its first abbess – is buried here. Inside the church are four marble columns supposedly from a Roman temple that once stood on the site. The vaulted choir dates from the 12th century, the nave was remodelled in the 15th century and the west front in the 18th. During the Revolution, the abbess was executed by guillotine, and the church fell into disuse. St-Pierre was reconsecrated in 1908. The tiny cemetery opens to the public only once a year, on 1 November.

Place du Tertre

📍 J1 🏠 75018 Ⓜ Abbesses

Tertre means "hillock", or mound, and this picturesque square is the highest point in Paris at 130 m (430 ft). It was once the site of the abbey gallows but is associated with artists, who began exhibiting paintings here in the 19th century. It is lined with colourful restaurants – La Mère Catherine dates back to 1793. In summer, the restaurant terraces spill out into the centre of the square. The house at No 21 was formerly the home of the irreverent "Free Commune," founded in 1920 to perpetuate the bohemian spirit of the area. The Old Montmartre information office is now here.

Cimetière de Montmartre

📍 G1 🏠 20 Ave Rachel 75018 📞 01 53 42 36 30 Ⓜ Place de Clichy, Blanche ⏰ 8am–6pm Mon–Fri, 8:30am–6pm Sat, 9am–6pm Sun (winter: to 5:30pm daily)

This has been the resting place for many artistic luminaries since the 19th century. The composers Hector Berlioz and Jacques Offenbach (who wrote the famous cancan tune) are buried here, alongside other celebrities such as La Goulue (stage name of Louise Weber, the cancan's first star performer and Toulouse-Lautrec's model), the painter Edgar Degas, writer Alexandre Dumas, German poet Heinrich Heine, Russian dancer Vaslav Nijinsky and film director François Truffaut. Cimetière de Montmartre is an evocative place, conveying the artistic creativity of the area a century ago with imaginative grave statues.

← The lively Place du Tertre with its many restaurants

To the east, close to Square Roland Dorgelès, is the often overlooked Cimetière St-Vincent. Here lie more of the great artistic names of the district, including Swiss composer Arthur Honegger and writer Marcel Aymé. Most notable is the grave of the great French painter Maurice Utrillo, one of the few famous Montmartre artists actually born in the area and many of whose works afford some of the most enduring images of the district.

Au Lapin Agile
📍J1 🏠22 Rue des Saules 75018 Ⓜ Lamarck-Caulaincourt 🕐9pm–1am Tue & Thu–Sun 🌐au-lapin-agile.com

The former Cabaret des Assassins derived its current name from a sign painted by the humorist André Gill. His picture of a rabbit escaping from a cooking pot (Le Lapin à Gill) is a pun on his own name. The club enjoyed popularity with intellectuals and artists at the start of the 20th century. Here in 1911, the novelist Roland Dorgelès and a group of other regulars staged one of the modern art world's most celebrated hoaxes, with the help of the café owner's donkey, Lolo. A paintbrush was tied to Lolo's tail, and the resulting daub was shown to critical acclaim at the Salon des Indépendants, under the title Sunset over the Adriatic, before the joke was revealed. In 1903, the premises were bought by the cabaret entrepreneur Aristide Bruand (painted in a series of posters by Toulouse-Lautrec). Years later, the cabaret venue manages to retain much of its original atmosphere.

St-Jean l'Évangéliste de Montmartre
📍H2 🏠19 Rue des Abbesses 75018 Ⓜ Abbesses 🕐9am–7pm Mon–Sat, 9:30am–6pm Sun (summer: to 7pm) 🌐saintjeandemontmartre.com

Designed by Anatole de Baudot and completed in 1904, this church was, controversially, the first to be built from reinforced concrete. The flower motifs on the interior are typical of the Art Nouveau style, while its interlocking arches suggest Islamic architecture. The red-brick facing has earned it the nickname St-Jean-des-Briques.

Place des Abbesses
📍H2 🏠75018 Ⓜ Abbesses

This is one of Paris's most picturesque squares. It is sandwiched between the rather dubious attractions of Place Pigalle, with its strip clubs, and Place du Tertre, which is mobbed by hundreds of tourists. Be sure not to miss the Abbesses Metro station with its green wrought-iron arches and amber lights. Designed by the architect Hector Guimard, it is one of the few surviving original Art Nouveau stations.

Halle St-Pierre
📍J1 🏠2 Rue Ronsard 75018 Ⓜ Anvers 🕐11am–6pm Mon–Sat (to 7pm Sat), noon–6pm Sun 🚫1 Jan, 1 May, 14 Jul, 15 Aug, Sat & Sun in Aug, 25 Dec 🌐hallesaintpierre.org

In 1945, the French painter Jean Dubuffet developed the concept of Art Brut (Outsider or Marginal Art) to describe works created outside the boundaries of "official" culture, often by psychiatric patients, prisoners and children. The Halle St-Pierre, at the foot of the Butte, is a museum and gallery devoted to these "raw" art forms. It also hosts avant-garde theatre and musical productions, holds literary evenings and debates and runs children's workshops. The collection includes more than 500 works of Naïve art collected by the publisher Max Fourny in the 1970s. There is also a specialist bookshop and café.

The Moulin Rouge, an iconic symbol of Parisian nightlife

Dalí Paris

📍 J1 🏠 11 Rue Poulbot 75018 Ⓜ Abbesses
🕙 10am–6pm daily
🚫 24 & 25 Dec 🌐 daliparis.com

A permanent exhibition of more than 300 works by the prolific painter and sculptor Salvador Dalí is displayed here in the heart of Montmartre. Through this impressive private collection – France's largest – of Dalí's Surrealist paintings, sculptures, engravings, objects and furniture, the dramatic character of the 20th-century Catalan genius comes to light. This fascinating museum also houses a commercial art gallery.

Musée de Montmartre

📍 J1 🏠 12 Rue Cortot 75018 Ⓜ Abbesses, Anvers 🕙 10am–6pm daily 🌐 museedemontmartre.fr

During the 17th century, this charming home belonged to the actor Rose de Rosimond (Claude de la Rose), a member of Molière's theatre company. From 1875, the big white house, undoubtedly the finest in Montmartre, provided living and studio space for artists, including Maurice Utrillo and his mother Suzanne Valadon, a former acrobat and model who became a talented

painter, as well as Raoul Dufy and Auguste Renoir.

The museum recounts the history of Montmartre through artifacts, drawings and photographs. It is particularly rich in memorabilia of bohemian life, and has a reconstruction of the Café de l'Abreuvoir, Utrillo's favourite watering hole. Valdon's studio-apartment was renovated and opened to the public in 2014, as was the Hôtel Demarne, which stages temporary exhibitions on Montmartre themes.

Moulin Rouge

📍 H2 🏠 82 Blvd de Clichy 75018 Ⓜ Blanche 🕙 Dinner: 7pm; shows: 9pm & 11pm daily 🌐 moulinrouge.fr

Built in 1885, the Moulin Rouge was turned into a dance hall as early as 1900. The cancan originated in Montparnasse, in the polka gardens of the Rue de la Grande-Chaumière, but it will always be associated with the Moulin

Rouge, where the wild and colourful dance shows were immortalized in the posters and drawings of Henri de Toulouse-Lautrec. The high-kicking routines of famous "Doriss girls" such as Yvette Guilbert and Jane Avril continue today in a glittering, Las Vegas-style revue that includes sophisticated light shows and displays of magic.

Moulin de la Galette

📍 H1 🏠 T-junction at Rue Tholozé and Rue Lepic 75018 Ⓜ Lamarck-Caulaincourt, Abbesses

Once, some 14 windmills dotted the Montmartre skyline and were used for grinding wheat and pressing grapes. Today, only two remain, both on Rue Lepic: the Radet, now above a restaurant confusingly named Moulin de la Galette and the reconstructed

Moulin de la Galette, originally built in 1622 and known as the Blute-fin. One of its mill owners, Debray, was supposedly crucified on one of the windmill's sails during the 1814 Siege of Paris. He had been trying to repulse the invading Cossacks. At the end of the 19th century, both mills became famous dance halls providing inspiration for many artists, notably Pierre-Auguste Renoir and Vincent van Gogh.

Rue Lepic runs steeply uphill from Montmartre's central shopping area. The Impressionist painter Armand Guillaumin once lived on the first floor of No 54. Van Gogh inhabited its third floor, and painted the view from there.

Rue des Martyrs

♀ J2 ♠ 75009 Ⓜ Pigalle

This quintessentially Parisian street owes its name to Saint Denis, who was martyred nearby. Rue des Martyrs retains much of the local, market-street vibe that has been lost in many similar locations in Paris. The street is full of tried-and-tested destinations adored by Parisians and visitors alike: pastry shops, restaurants, cafés, and even a boutique dedicated to salted-butter caramel. A few recognizable brands pop up here and

there, but overall the street is one of the most individual and fashionable in Paris.

Batignolles

♀ F1 ♠ 75007 Ⓜ Place de Clichy, Rome, Brochant

Formerly used as a royal hunting ground, this neighbourhood in the 17th arrondissement of northwestern Paris later grew into a small hamlet. Although it officially became part of the city in the second half of the 19th century, it still feels like a small French village. In the 19th century, the area had a lively cultural vibe and counted among its residents the painter Edouard Manet and his fellow artists (who became known as the Groupe des Batignolles), the writer Émile Zola and, later, the Belgian singer Jacques Brel.

The lovely Ste-Marie des Batignolles church sits in the heart of the neighbourhood. While Batignolles has a calm, community feel, it also has a slightly urban atmosphere, with a good mix of well-frequented bars, stylish boutiques and restaurants. It was one of the first areas in Paris to label its up-and-coming class of residents *bobos*, a short-hand term for "bourgeois bohemians".

Two markets are held in the area: the organic Marché

Biologique des Batignolles on Boulevard des Batignolles and the covered market on Rue Lemercier, which dates back to 1846. At weekends, families converge on the area's several parks, the two largest being the Square des Batignolles and the Parc Clichy – Martin-Luther-King, which features playgrounds, duck ponds, a skate park and running trails. The district has undergone substantial development in recent years, and there are modern flats, shops and office buildings, including the new Paris law courts.

OPÉRA AND GRANDS BOULEVARDS

Studded with theatres and crowned by the Opéra Garnier, this district epitomizes Baron Haussmann's plans for Paris, with monuments at every intersection. Its broad avenues, lined with exquisite churches and wallet-emptying department stores, attract Parisians and camera-toting tourists alike. This is the place to stroll, shop and repeat, whether it's for rose-flavoured *macarons* from Ladurée's original shop or a luxury bag from Printemps.

↓ Galeries Lafayette department store

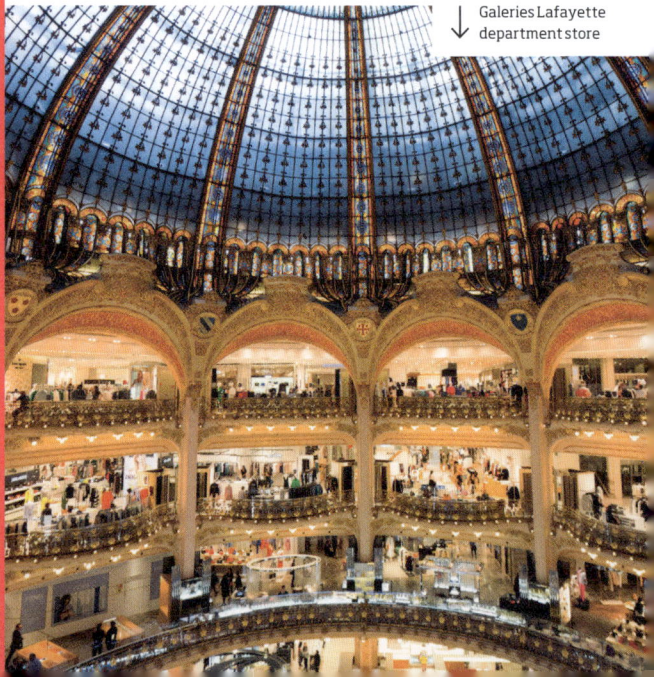

Opéra National
de Paris Garnier, one of
Paris's most-visited sights

Did You Know?

Underneath the building
is a small lake, which
inspired the phantom's
hiding place in *Phantom
of the Opera*.

OPÉRA NATIONAL
DE PARIS GARNIER

📍H4 🏛️Pl de l'Opéra 75009 Ⓜ️Opéra 🕐Aug–mid-Jul: 10am–5pm daily (last adm:
4:15pm); box office: Aug–mid-Jul: 11am–4pm daily 🚫For daytime performances,
1 Jan, 1 May, 25 Dec (check website for exceptional closures) 🌐operadeparis.fr

**Sometimes compared to a giant wedding cake, this palatial opera house with
its ornate interior is a sumptuous setting in which to enjoy a ballet or opera.**

The building was designed by Charles
Garnier for Napoleon III; construction
started in 1862 and finished in 1875 after
interruptions from the Prussian War and
1871 uprising. Its unique appearance is due
to a mixture of materials (including stone,
marble and bronze) and styles, ranging from
Classical to Baroque, with many columns,
friezes and sculptures on the exterior.

Behind the flat-topped foyer, the cupola
sits above the auditorium, while the triangular pediment that rises up behind the
cupola marks the front of the stage. Don't
miss the splendid Grand Staircase, made
of white marble with a balustrade of red
and green marble, and the Grand Foyer, its
domed ceiling covered with mosaics. The
five-tiered auditorium is a riot of red velvet,
plaster cherubs and gold leaf. The false
ceiling was painted by Marc Chagall in 1964.

Operas are performed both here and
at the Opéra National de Paris Bastille
but the Paris Opera Ballet predominantly
remains here.

EXPERIENCE MORE

Place de la Madeleine

F4 75008
Madeleine
Flower market: 9am–8pm Mon-Sat

The Place de la Madeleine was created at the same time as the Madeleine church. The square hosts a number of upmarket restaurants, cafés and speciality food shops, including Maille at No 6, famous for its mustards. The large house at No 9 on nearby Boulevard Malesherbes, just off Place de la Madeleine, is where Marcel Proust spent his childhood. To the east of La Madeleine are a small flower market and some beautifully renovated 19th-century Art Nouveau public toilets.

La Madeleine

G4 Pl de la Madeleine 75008
Madeleine 9:30am–7pm daily eglise-la madeleine.com

This church, dedicated to Mary Magdalene, is one of the best-known buildings in Paris because of its prominent location and great size. It stands facing south to Place de la Concorde and is the architectural counterpoint of the Palais Bourbon (home of the French Parliament) across the river. It was started in 1764 but construction halted with the onset of the Revolution in 1789. After the battle of Jena (Iéna) in 1806, Napoleon decided to build a temple dedicated to military glory and commissioned Pierre Vignon to design it. The church was finished in 1842.

A colonnade of Corinthian columns encircles the building and supports a sculptured frieze. The bas-reliefs on the bronze doors by Henri de Triqueti show the Ten Commandments. The interior is decorated with marble and gilt, and has some fine sculpture, notably François Rude's *Baptism of Christ*. The church has a rich musical tradition; Gabriel Fauré and Camille Saint-Saëns were both organists here. Concerts, especially choral and organ recitals, take place regularly. The funerals of many celebrities have taken place here, including that of Frédéric Chopin, Edith Piaf, Charles Trenet and Johnny Hallyday.

Did You Know?

The flower market at Place de la Madeleine has sold colourful bouquets since the early 1800s.

Église Ste-Trinité

G3 Place d'Estienne d'Orves 75009 Trinité-d'Estienne d'Orves 7:15am–7:45pm Mon-Fri, 10am–7:30pm Sat, 9:30am–8:15pm Sun latriniteparis.com

Inspired by Renaissance-era Italian churches, this 19th-century masterpiece was consecrated in 1913.

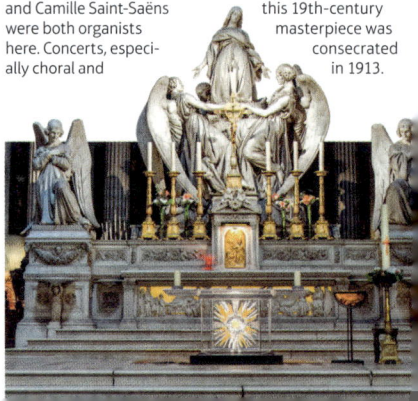

The church, often referred to simply as La Trinité, is the monumental centrepiece of the busy Place d'Estienne d'Orves intersection, created by Baron Haussmann.

As part of his grand project to redesign Paris, Haussmann moved the church a few hundred metres from its original location. The church is beautifully decorated with a large belfry. Inside, each chapel reveals a rich series of paintings and decorations celebrating saints such as local favourites Geneviève and Vincent de Paul.

Théâtre Mogador

G3 **25 Rue de Mogador 75009** **Trinité-d'Estienne d'Orves** **theatremogador.com**

The Théâtre Mogador was built by London theatre mogul Alfred Butt. It was inaugurated in 1919 by future American president Franklin Delano Roosevelt. Numerous politicians were in town to negotiate the Treaty of Versailles after World War I, so taking in a show must have seemed like a good idea. It once

←

The ornate high altar of the Église de la Madeleine

hosted operettas and Sergei Diaghilev's Ballets Russes, but has also staged classic musicals such as *Hello, Dolly!* and *Les Misérables*. Now, this three-tier theatre produces mostly big-budget Broadway shows in French, such as *The Lion King* and *The Producers*.

Galeries Lafayette

H4 **40 Blvd Haussmann 75009** **Chaussée d'Antin-Lafayette** **10am-8:30pm Mon-Sat, 11am-8pm Sun** **haussmann.galerieslafayette.com**

Dating back to 1893, this charming store is a Parisian icon and an essential stop on any visit to the city. The massive complex includes men's and women's fashion, a homewares department and a gourmet food hall. At Christmas, a massive tree fills the Art Nouveau cupola, while the windows tell whimsical holiday stories popular with kids.

Anyone can take the escalator to the rooftop terrace, where spectacular views of the city await. The store can become a madhouse during the biannual sales, the *soldes*, but it's all part of the Galeries Lafayette experience.

EAT

La Petite Régalade

The chef offers an innovative take on *la pascade*, a crêpe-like dish filled with gourmet ingredients.

G4 **14 Rue Daunou 75002** **Sun** **lapetiteregalade.com**

€€€

Chartier

This old workers' canteen is still a budget favourite for French classics.

J4 **7 Rue du Faubourg Montmartre 75009** **bouillon-chartier.com**

€€€

DRINK

Harry's New York Bar

Birthplace of the Bloody Mary – and other cocktails – it's tradition to make a stop here.

H4 **5 Rue Daunou 75002** **harrysbar.fr**

Gare St-Lazare

📍 G3 🏠 13 Rue d'Amsterdam 75008
Ⓜ Gare Saint-Lazare

One of Europe's second-busiest train stations, the Gare St-Lazare is probably the most celebrated in art. Opened in 1837, it sends trains to the station closest to Giverny, where Claude Monet painted his famous *Water Lilies*. The artist was just one of many 19th-century painters to immortalize the St-Lazare station in his works.

Renowned painters Caillebotte and Manet also lived near the station, and their depictions of it hang in galleries around the world. The station houses a shopping mall with more than 80 shops, as well as a number of restaurants and bars.

Printemps

📍 G4 🏠 64 Blvd Haussmann 75009
Ⓜ Havre Caumartin, Haussmann St-Lazare
🕐 10am–8pm Mon, Tue & Thu–Sat, 11am–8pm Wed & Sun 🌐 printemps.com

A stunning Art Nouveau palace dedicated to shopping, the Printemps department store dates back to 1865. High fashion fills the floors, and it feels slightly more elegant and refined than neighbouring Galeries Lafayette. The restaurant under the massive stained-glass dome is a resplendent spot for lunch, while the rooftop café offers great views of the Sacré-Coeur.

Église St-Augustin

📍 F3 🏠 8 Ave César Caire 75008 Ⓜ St-Augustin
🕐 8:30am–7pm Mon–Fri, 9am–12:30pm & 2:30–7:30pm Sat, 8:30am–12:30pm & 4:30–8pm Sun
🌐 saintaugustin.net

This church is located in one of the most exclusive neighbourhoods in Paris. Designed by Victor Baltard, the architect of Les Halles, and completed in 1868 at the intersection of sweeping new boulevards, the building initially drew criticism for its oversized dome and curious red turret. Large quantities of metal were used in the church's construction, and its cast iron framework provides a decorative feature of the interior,

← A rooftop view of the Art Nouveau Printemps department store

complete with iron angels at the tops of the pillars.

Musée Grévin

📍 J4 🏛 10 Blvd Montmartre 75009
Ⓜ Grands Boulevards
🕐 Hours vary, check website 🅦 grevin-paris.com

This waxworks museum was founded in 1882 and is now a Paris landmark, on a par with Madame Tussauds in London. It contains tableaux of vivid historical scenes (such as the arrest of Louis XVI), the Palais des Mirages (a giant walk-in kaleidoscope) and the Cabinet Fantastique, which features regular conjuring shows given by a live magician. Famous figures from the worlds of art, sport and politics are also on show, with new celebrities constantly replacing faded and forgotten stars.

Le Grand Rex

📍 K4 🏛 1 Blvd Poissonnière 75002
Ⓜ Bonne Nouvelle
🅦 legrandrex.com

A national monument, as well as an innovative example of Art Deco

architecture, Le Grand Rex, built in 1932, was long touted as Europe's most opulent cinema, hosting many red-carpet events. One of the largest of its kind in Europe, the Grand Rex is a fading but beautiful symbol of the history of cinema. The auditorium has a starred ceiling, and a huge screen. Every December since 1954, the cinema has hosted the Féerie des Eaux, a family-film event featuring an onstage water show.

Chapelle Expiatoire

📍 F4 🏛 29 Rue Pasquier 75008 Ⓜ St-Augustin
📞 01 42 65 35 80 🕐 Apr-Sep: 10am-12:30pm & 1:30-6:30pm Tue-Sat; Oct-Mar: 10am-12:30pm & 1:30-5pm 🅦 chapelle-expiatoire-paris.fr

King Louis XVIII dedicated this chapel in 1816 to the memory of his brother King Louis XVI and sister-in-law Marie-Antoinette. The pair were buried in a cemetery here after being guillotined nearby at Place de la Concorde. The mass grave, known as the Madeleine Cemetery, was one of four to hold the remains of guillotine victims. Marie-

Antoinette and Louis XVI were moved to the Basilica of St-Denis in the 19th century. The chapel merely hints at this turbulent history with a modest Neo-Classical memorial. The tiny garden contains cenotaphs to those who were buried here, including victims of the fireworks disaster at Marie and Louis's wedding in 1770.

→ A statue of Marie-Antoinette in the Chapelle Expiatoire

LOUVRE AND LES HALLES

Paris's former royal palace and central market are as lively as ever. The Musée du Louvre, with its infamous glass pyramid and the *Mona Lisa*, needs no introduction. The stately manicured gardens of the adjacent Tuileries house cafés and other art galleries. Les Halles was historically the hub of food distribution in the city, and the smells of ripened cheeses and fresh baguettes still tempt shoppers along Rue Montorgueil. It's all about cuisine here, from fine dining to street food, and wine bars and cocktail clubs shake up the nights.

↓ The iconic glass pyramid of the Louvre

↑ Admiring art in the
Musée du Louvre

MUSÉE DU LOUVRE

📍H6 🏛Pl du Louvre Ⓜ Palais-Royal-Musée du Louvre 🚌21, 27, 39, 68, 69, 72, 81, 95 🚉Châtelet-Les-Halles 🚇Louvre 🕐9am-6pm Wed-Mon (to 9:45pm Fri) 📅1 Jan, 1 May, 25 Dec 🌐louvre.fr

First opened to the public in 1793 after the Revolution, the Louvre contains one of the most important art collections in the world.

Constructed as a fortress in 1190 by King Philippe-Auguste to protect Paris against Viking raids, the Louvre lost its imposing keep during the reign of François I (1514–47), who replaced it with a Renaissance-style building. Thereafter, four centuries of French kings and emperors improved and enlarged it. A glass pyramid designed by IM Pei was added to the main courtyard in 1989, from which all of the galleries can be reached.

The Louvre's treasures can be traced back to the 16th-century collection of François I, who purchased many Italian paintings, including the *Mona Lisa (La Gioconda)*. At the time of Louis XIV's reign (1643–1715) there were a mere 200 works, but donations and purchases augmented the collection and it has been continually enriched ever since.

GALLERY GUIDE

There are nine departments spread across four floors: Near Eastern antiquities; Egyptian antiquities; Greek, Etruscan and Roman antiquities; Islamic art; sculptures; paintings; and prints and drawings.

Must See

EXPERIENCE MORE

Musée de l'Orangerie

📍F6 🏛Jardin des Tuileries, Pl de la Concorde 75001 Ⓜ Concorde ⏰9am–6pm Wed–Mon; advance booking recommended 🗓1 May, 14 Jul am & 25 Dec 🌐musee-orangerie.fr

Claude Monet's crowning work, the water lily series, or *Nymphéas*, can be found here. The series was painted in his garden at Giverny, near Paris, and presented to the public in 1927. These superb large-scale canvases are complemented well by the outstanding Walter-Guillaume collection of artists of the École de Paris, from the late-Impressionist era to the inter-War period. This is a remarkable concentration of masterpieces, including a room of dramatic works by Soutine and some 14 works by Cézanne – still lifes, portraits *(Madame Cézanne)* and landscapes, such as *Dans le Parc du Château Noir.*

Pierre-Auguste Renoir is represented by 27 canvases, including *Les Fillettes au Piano (Young Girls at the Piano).* There are early Picassos, works by Henri Rousseau – notably *La Carriole du Père Junier (Old Junier's Cart)* – and Matisse, and a portrait of Paul Guillaume by Modigliani. All are bathed in the natural light that flows through the windows. Temporary exhibitions are shown on the lower ground floor.

Galerie Vivienne

📍J5 🏛4 Rue des Petits Champs 75002 Ⓜ Bourse, Pyramides ⏰Generally 8:30am–8:30pm daily 🌐galerie-vivienne.com

The early 19th century saw the rise of fashionable covered *passages*, reminiscent of the souks explored dur-ing Napoleon's conquests in North Africa. At the height of their popularity there were over 100 of them; they were the shopping malls of their day, well before the department stores came of age.

Galerie Vivienne, built in 1823, was a particularly sumptuous example of such a *passage.* Its lovely décor has been restored, including its atrium ceilings and mosaic floor with patterns reminiscent of decorations from Pompeii. It's the perfect all-weather retreat for a glass of wine, a little bit of shopping in the elegant boutiques, or browsing in the Librairie Jousseaume second-hand bookshop.

Daniel Buren's columns in the courtyard of the Jardin du Palais-Royal

Neighbouring Galerie Colbert has no shops (it houses various cultural institutions) but is equally elegant and worth a peek for its lovely glass rotunda.

Jardin du Palais-Royal

📍H5 🏛6 Rue de Montpensier, Pl du Palais-Royal 75001 Ⓜ Palais-Royal ⏰Hours vary, check website 🌐domaine-palais-royal.fr

The current garden is about one-third smaller than the original one, laid out by the royal gardener for Cardinal Richelieu in the 1630s. This is due to the construction, between 1781 and 1784, of 60 uniform houses bordering three sides of the square. Today, restaurants, art galleries and specialist shops line the square, which has numbered Jean Marais, Jean Cocteau and Colette among its famous former residents.

The courtyard contains the controversial black-and-white striped stone columns that form conceptual artist Daniel Buren's *Les Deux Plateaux.* The columns were installed in the pedestrianized Palais-Royal courtyard

in 1986, despite vociferous opposition about their suitability for the space. Today, they are loved by children and skateboarders.

Bourse de Commerce - Pinault Collection

📍 J6 **🏠** 2 Rue de Viarmes 75001 **Ⓜ** Louvre-Rivoli, Les Halles **🕐** 11am-7pm Wed-Mon (to 9pm Fri); tours (in English): 1:30pm & 3pm daily **📅** 1 May **🌐** pinaultcollection.com

A former grain market and then Commodities Exchange, this glass-domed circular building dates to 1767. It was later transformed into an exhibition space, housing the art collection of billionaire businessman François Pinault. Over 10,000 artworks, including pieces by Damien Hirst and George and Bridget Riley, are displayed in rotation. As well as changing exhibitions, there are concerts, screenings and conferences. The top-floor café-restaurant,

La Halle aux Grains, run by the Michelin-starred Bras brothers, has wonderful views over the city.

Tour Jean Sans Peur

📍 K5 **🏠** 20 Rue Étienne-Marcel 75002 **Ⓜ** Étienne-Marcel, Sentier **🕐** 1:30-6pm Wed-Sun **🌐** tourjeansanspeursite.word press.com

The Duc de Bourgogne feared reprisals after the Duc d'Orléans was assassinated on his orders in 1408. To protect himself, he had this 27-m (88-ft) tower built onto his home, the Hôtel de Bourgogne, and moved his bedroom up to the fourth floor (reached by a flight of 140 steps). The fine vaulted ceiling is decorated with stone carvings of oak leaves, hawthorn and hops, symbols of the Burgundys.

Ô Chateau

📍 J5 **🏠** 68 Rue Jean-Jacques Rousseau 75001 **Ⓜ** Louvre-Rivoli, Étienne Marcel **🕐** Hours vary, check website **🌐** o-chateau.com

With 50 wines served by the glass, this wine-tasting bar in the heart of Les Halles is one of the best places to learn about your soon-to-be favourite vintages. Stop in for a few drinks, or take a class or even a trip. They can organize outings to Champagne for tastings or prepare a multi-course meal served in one of their vaulted dining rooms. A sommelier pairs each dish with wine, explaining the particularities of French viticulture. English-speakers are catered for, so there's no chance of losing anything in translation.

← Statues set into the façade of the Gothic church of St-Merry

The 105 years (1532–1637) it took to complete the church saw the flowering of the Renaissance style, which is evident in the church's magnificent pillars, arches and columns. The stained-glass windows in the chancel are created from cartoons by Philippe de Champaigne.

Molière was buried in this church; and the Marquise de Pompadour, official mistress of Louis XV, was baptized here, as was Cardinal Richelieu. Don't miss a chance to hear the fine organ at one of the regular recitals that take place.

St-Merry

📍 K7 🏠 76 Rue de la Verrerie 75004 Ⓜ Hôtel de Ville 🕐 8am-8pm Mon-Sat, 9am-1pm & 3:30-6pm Sun 🌐 saintmerry.org

The site of this church dates back to the 7th century. St Médéric, the abbot of St-Martin d'Autun, was buried here at the beginning of the 8th century; he died while on pilgrimage in Paris. Construction of the church – in the Flamboyant Gothic style – took place in 1500–1550.

The west front is especially rich in decoration, and the northwest turret contains the oldest bell in Paris, dating from 1331. St-Merry was the wealthy parish church of the Lombard moneylenders, who gave their name to the nearby Rue des Lombards. Concerts, usually choral or piano, are held every Sunday afternoon.

St-Eustache

📍 J6 🏠 2 Impasse St-Eustache, Pl du Jour 75001 Ⓜ Les Halles 🚇 Châtelet-Les-Halles 🕐 9:30am-7pm Mon-Fri, 10am-7pm Sat, 9am-7pm Sun 🌐 saint-eustache.org

With its Gothic plan and Renaissance decoration, St-Eustache is one of the most beautiful churches in Paris. Its interior layout is modelled on Notre-Dame, with five naves and side and radial chapels.

Westfield Forum des Halles

📍 J6 🏠 101 Porte Berger 75001 Ⓜ Les Halles, Châtelet 🚇 Châtelet-Les-Halles 🕐 Complex: 10am-8:30pm Mon-Sat, 11am-7pm Sun; restaurants & cinema: 9am-11:30pm daily 🌐 forum deshalles.com

Known simply as Les Halles and built amid controversy on the site of a famous produce market, this vast complex, much of it underground, is covered by an undulating glass-and-steel roof known as "La Canopée". Restaurants and shops abound, and there is a multiplex cinema, a gym and swimming pool, and a cinema resource centre, the Forum des Images. Here, you can choose from thousands of cinema, television and amateur films, many featuring footage of the city of Paris. Above ground are peaceful gardens, pergolas and pretty mini-pavilions.

Fontaine des Innocents

⊙ K6 ⌂ Pl Joachim-du-Bellay 75001 Ⓜ Les Halles ⒭ Châtelet-es-Halles

This carefully restored Renaissance fountain is a popular meeting place and a Les Halles landmark. It stands in the Place Joachim-du-Bellay, the area's main crossroads. Erected in 1549 on the Rue St-Denis, it was moved to its present location in the 18th century, when the square was constructed on the site of a former graveyard. Originally set into a wall, the fountain had only three sides so a fourth had to be con-

structed. It is decorated with mythological figures.

Jeu de Paume

⊙ F5 ⌂ Jardin des Tuileries, 1 Pl de la Concorde 75008 Ⓜ Concorde ⏱ 11am–7pm Tue–Sun (to 9pm Tue) 🗓 1 Jan, 1 May, 14 Jul, 25 Dec and in between exhibitions ⓦ jeudepaume.org

The Jeu de Paume – or real tennis court – was built by Napoleon III in 1851. When real (royal) tennis was replaced in popularity by lawn tennis, the court was used to exhibit art. Eventually, an Impressionist museum was founded here. In 1986, the collection moved to Musée d'Orsay. The Jeu de Paume now shows exhibitions of contemporary

photography as well as film and video installations from both established and emerging artists.

Arc de Triomphe du Carrousel

⊙ H6 ⌂ Pl du Carrousel 75001 Ⓜ Palais-Royal

Built by Napoleon in 1806–8 as an entrance to the former Palais des Tuileries, this vast pink marble arch, inspired by ancient Roman triumphal arches, was originally topped by the so-called Horses of St Mark's which Napoleon had looted from Venice's St Mark's Cathedral. The original sculptures were returned in 1815 after Napoleon's defeat at the Battle of Waterloo and replaced by copies.

→

Impressive façade of the Jeu de Paume

EIFFEL TOWER
AND INVALIDES

This corner of town is grandiose and ornate, with the gold-topped Les Invalides soaring against the skyline. Full of history and artifacts, it plays second fiddle to the neighbourhood's real star: the Iron Lady herself, the Eiffel Tower, rising at the edge of the river. Away from the chaos of tours and elevator queues, this district also offers quaint streets such as Rue Cler where colourful, buttery pastries await. Some of the city's top restaurants aren't far away. If Michelin stars seem overly excessive then a picnic on the Champ-de-Mars underneath the tower will do, with the appropriate bottle of oaky red wine, of course.

The Eiffel Tower illuminated at night ↓

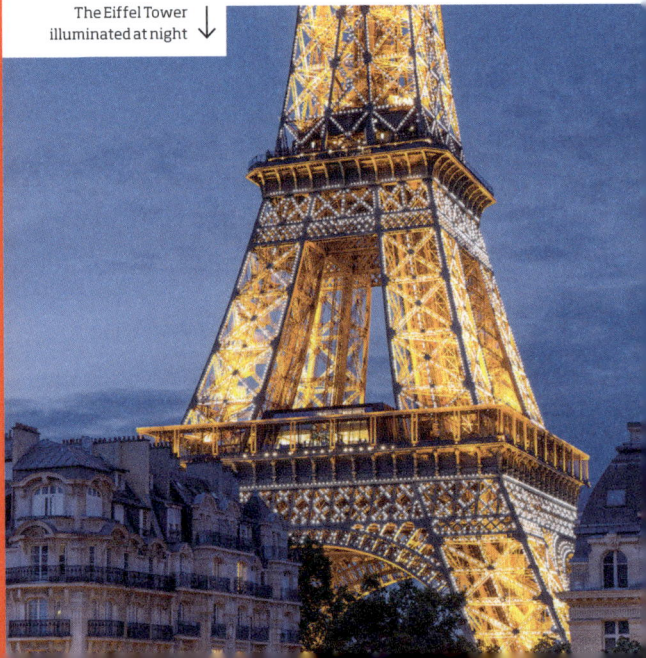

↑ The view from the tower, ranging up to 72 km (45 miles)

EIFFEL TOWER

📍 B7 🏠 Quai Branly and Champ-de-Mars 75007
Ⓜ Bir Hakeim 🚌 30, 42, 69, 82 to Champ-de-Mars
🚇 Champ-de-Mars-Tour Eiffel ⏰ Sep-Jun: 9:30am–11:45pm daily (6:30pm for stairs); Jul-Aug: 9am–12:45am daily 🗓 14 Jul 🌐 toureiffel.paris

An impressive feat of engineering and the most distinctive symbol of Paris, the Eiffel Tower stands 324 m (1,063 ft) tall and offers unrivalled views over the city.

Originally built to impress visitors to the 1889 Exposition Universelle, the Eiffel Tower (Tour Eiffel) was meant to be a temporary addition to the Paris skyline. Built by the engineer Gustave Eiffel, it was fiercely decried by 19th-century aesthetes – the author Guy de Maupassant frequently ate lunch at the tower as it was the only place he could avoid seeing it. The world's tallest structure until 1931, when New York's Empire State Building was completed, the tower attracts almost seven million visitors a year. The glass-floored first level houses a modern visitors' centre and an interactive museum chronicling the history of the tower. Book tickets ahead of time to avoid long queues.

THE TOWER IN FIGURES

276 m (905 ft): the height of the viewing gallery on the third level

1,665: the number of steps to the third level

2.5 million: the number of rivets holding the tower together

7 cm (2.5 in): the maximum amount that the tower ever sways

10,100 tonnes: the tower's total weight

60 tonnes: the amount of paint needed to decorate the ironwork

18 cm (7 in): how far the top can move in a curve under the effect of heat

Must See

← Jean Nouvel's elegant building, an exhibit in itself, from the inside

MUSÉE DU QUAI BRANLY– JACQUES CHIRAC

📍 C6 🏠 37 Quai Branly 75007 Ⓜ Alma-Marceau, Bir-Hakeim, Iéna 🚌 42, 63, 72, 80, 82, 92 🚆 Pont de l'Alma 🕙 10:30am–7pm Tue–Sun (to 10pm Thu) 📅 Mon (except during all school hols besides summer hols), 1 May, 25 Dec 🌐 quaibranly.fr

This rich collection of artifacts from Africa, Asia, Oceania and the Americas resides in a striking building that uses surrounding greenery as a natural backdrop to the art.

🔍 HIDDEN GEM
Key Object

The Africa collection houses a striking 1.91 m (6 ft 3 in) androgynous wooden statue from Mali, which combines a regal male head with a woman's breasts.

Widely regarded as former President Jacques Chirac's legacy to Paris's cultural scene, quai Branly has proved a major tourist pull since it opened in 2006. The stylish Jean Nouvel building displays 3,500 exhibits from the French state's vast non-Western art collection, one of the world's most prolific. Items include an array of African instruments, Gabonese masks, Aztec statues and painted animal hides from North America. Outside, the grounds offer visitors breathing space, and in summer the museum's 500-seat auditorium opens onto an outdoor theatre for music and dance. The rooftop restaurant offers breathtaking views.

DÔME DES INVALIDES

📍 E7 🏠 6 Blvd des Invalides, Esplanade des Invalides 75007 Ⓜ La Tour-Maubourg, Varenne 🚌 28, 63, 69, 80, 82, 83, 87, 92, 93 to Les Invalides
🚆 Invalides Ⓣ Tour Eiffel 🕐 10am–6pm daily (to 10pm first Fri of the month)
🚫 1 Jan, 1 May, 25 Dec 🌐 musee-armee.fr

Built in the French Classical style on the orders of Louis XIV, this ornate church houses the tombs of Napoleon Bonaparte and a host of other great French military men. Its magnificent dome is a landmark on the city skyline and glistens as much now as it did when the Sun King had it first gilded in 1715.

The Dôme des Invalides was designed in 1676 by Jules Hardouin-Mansart for the exclusive use of Louis XIV and for the location of royal tombs. Slotted among the existing buildings of the Invalides military complex, the resulting master-piece complements the surrounding structures and is one of the greatest examples of 17th-century French architecture. After Louis XIV's death, plans to bury the royal family in the church were abandoned, and it became a monument to Bourbon glory. In 1840, Louis-Philippe decided to install Napoleon's remains in the crypt, and the addition of the tombs of Vauban, Marshal Foch and other figures of military prominence have since turned this church into a French military memorial.

NAPOLEON'S RETURN

King Louis-Philippe decided to bring the Emperor Napoleon's body back from St Helena as a gesture of reconciliation to the Republican and Bonapartist parties contesting his regime. The Dôme des Invalides, with its historical and military associations, was an obvious choice for Napoleon's final resting place. His body was encased in six coffins and finally placed in the crypt in 1861, at the culmination of a grand ceremony which was attended by Napoleon III.

←

Napoleon's tomb at the Dôme des Invalides

EXPERIENCE MORE

Hôtel des Invalides

📍E7 🏛6 Blvd des Invalides, Esplanade des Invalides 75007 Ⓜ️La Tour-Maubourg, Varenne ℝℰℝInvalides 🕙10am–6pm daily (to 10pm first Fri of the month) 🚫1 Jan, 1 May, 25 Dec 🌐musee-armee.fr

Founded by Louis XIV, the Hôtel des Invalides was France's first military hospital. Designed by Libéral Bruand and completed in 1675, it became home to French war veterans and disabled soldiers who, prior to its inauguration, had been reduced to begging on the streets.

Today, the Classical façade is one of the most impressive sights in Paris, with its four storeys, the bank of cannons in the forecourt, garden and tree-lined esplanade that stretches to the Seine.

Part of the building is still home to veterans. The south side leads to St-Louis-des-Invalides, the soldiers' church, which backs on to the magnificent Dôme des Invalides of Jules Hardouin-Mansart. The dome was regilded in 1989.

Musée de l'Armée

📍E7 🏛Hôtel des Invalides, 129 Rue de Grenelle, 75007 (wheelchair access at 6 Blvd des Invalides) Ⓜ️La Tour-Maubourg, Varenne ℝℰℝInvalides 🕙10am–6pm daily (to 10pm first Fri of the month) 🚫1 Jan, 1 May, 25 Dec 🌐musee-armee.fr

This is one of the world's most comprehensive museums of military history, with fascinating exhibits ranging from the Stone Age to the fall of the Berlin Wall. Situated in the northeast refectory, the Ancient Armoury department is worth visiting for the collection on display, one of the largest in the world, as much as for the 17th-century murals by Joseph Parrocel adorning the walls. These celebrate Louis XIV's military conquests.

The life of Charles de Gaulle and his role in World War II are documented in the *Historial de Gaulle*, a film and interactive multimedia attraction (closed Mon). The Département Moderne is in two parts: the first (1640–1792) covers the reign of Louis XIV, while the second (1792–1871) displays a collection of Napoleon's mementos. Items include his campaign bed, sword and his stuffed dog.

Rue Cler

📍D7 🏛75007 Ⓜ️École Militaire, La Tour-Maubourg

This is a typically charming Parisian market street, albeit one chic enough

←

The splendid Hôtel des Invalides seen from Pont Alexandre III

for the 7th arrondissement, the richest district in Paris. The bulk of senior civil servants, wealthy expatriates, business leaders and many diplomats live in this residential neighbourhood. Most of the food and drink stores – selling not just fresh produce but also cheese, chocolates, ice creams, patisseries and charcuterie – are gathered along the cobblestoned stretch south of Rue de Grenelle.

Musée Rodin

🗺 E7 🏠 79 Rue de Varenne 75007 🚇 Varenne 🕙 10am-6:30pm Tue-Sun; advance booking recommended 📅 1 Jan, 1 May, 25 Dec 🌐 musee-rodin.fr

Auguste Rodin, widely regarded as one of the greatest French sculptors of the 19th century, lived and worked in the elegant 18th-century Hôtel Biron from 1908 until his death in 1917. In return for a state-owned flat and studio, Rodin agreed to leave his artworks to the nation.

Some 300 works from Rodin's collection can now be seen in the museum. The attractive grounds consist of a rose garden, an ornamental garden and a relaxation area with benches, and

contain some of Rodin's most celebrated sculptures: *The Gates of Hell*, *The Burghers of Calais*, *Balzac* and *The Thinker*. Spread across 18 rooms, the museum combines a chronology of Rodin's creative development with a thematic exploration of his workshop. It has even re-created a space exactly as it was when Rodin lived and worked here. The outdoor café makes a lovely spot for a drink in warmer weather.

Musée des Égouts

🗺 D6 🏠 Pl Habib Bourguiba, opposite 93 Quai d'Orsay 75007 🚇 Alma-Marceau 🚆 Pont de l'Alma 🕙 10am-5pm Tue-Sun 📅 1 Jan, 1 May, 25 Dec 🌐 musee-egouts.paris.fr

One of Baron Haussmann's finest achievements, the majority of Paris's *égouts* sewers date from the Second Empire (1852–70). In the 20th century, surprisingly the sewers became a popular attraction. The Musée des Égouts allows visitors to tour the small area around the Quai d'Orsay entrance. Display boards explain the history of Paris's water supply and waste management. It is a good idea to book guided tours well in advance.

EAT

Le P'tit Troquet

This cosy little restaurant offers classic French dishes.

🗺 D7 🏠 28 Rue de l'Exposition 75007 📅 Sat, Sun 🌐 leptittroquet.fr

€€€

David Toutain

Visit this beloved restaurant for creative, two-star Michelin dining in a relaxed setting.

🗺 E6 🏠 29 Rue Surcouf 75007 📅 Sat, Sun 🌐 davidtoutain.com

€€€

Arpège

Alain Passard's three-star restaurant is a worthwhile treat. Dishes are prepared using produce from the restaurant's kitchen garden.

🗺 F7 🏠 84 Rue de Varenne 75007 📅 Sat, Sun 🌐 alain-passard.com

€€€

St-Louis-des-Invalides

♀ E7 **🏠 Hôtel des Invalides, 129 Rue de Grenelle 75007** **Ⓜ La Tour-Maubourg, Varenne** **🚆 Invalides** **🕐 10am–6pm daily (Nov-Mar: to 5pm)** **📅 1 Jan, 1 May, 25 Dec** **🌐 musee-armee.fr**

The "soldiers' church" was built in 1679–1708 by Jules Hardouin-Mansart from original designs by Libéral Bruand. The imposing but stark interior is decorated with banners seized in battle.

The first performance of Berlioz's *Requiem* was given on the fine 17th-century organ in 1837, with an orchestra accompanied by a battery of outside artillery.

Champ-de-Mars

♀ C7 **🏠 75007** **Ⓜ École Militaire** **🚆 Champ de Mars-Tour Eiffel**

The gardens stretching from the Eiffel Tower to the École Militaire were originally a parade ground for the officer cadets of the École Militaire. The area has since been used for horse-racing, hot-air balloon ascents and the mass celebrations for 14 July, the anniversary of the Revolution. The first Bastille Day ceremony was held in 1790 in the presence of a glum,

captive Louis XVI. Vast exhibitions were held here in the late 19th century, including the 1889 World Fair for which the Eiffel Tower was erected. *Le Mur de la Paix*, Clara Halter and Jean-Michel Wilmotte's symbolic monument to world peace, stands at one end.

The park is popular with Parisian families and tourists, who come here to relax, walk their dogs (it is one of the few parks in Paris where dogs are allowed) and to participate in the numerous activities for children, which include playgrounds, pony rides, puppet shows and a carousel. There is also an outdoor café.

Ste-Clotilde

♀ F7 **🏠 23B Rue las Cases 75007** **Ⓜ Solférino, Varenne, Invalides** **🕐 9am-7:30pm Mon-Fri, 10am-8pm Sat & Sun (Jul & Aug: hours vary, check website)** **📅 Non-religious public hols** **🌐 sainte-clotilde.com**

Designed by the German architect François-Christian Gau and the first of its kind to be built in Paris, this church, in Neo-Gothic style,

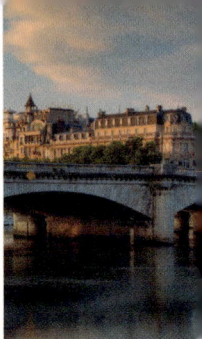

→

Assemblée Nationale on the Left Bank of the Seine

was inspired by the mid-19th-century enthusiasm for the Middle Ages, made fashionable by such writers as Victor Hugo.

The church is noted for its imposing twin towers, visible from across the Seine, and there are sculptures of the Stations of the Cross inside. The composer César Franck was the organist here.

Assemblée Nationale Palais-Bourbon

♀ F6 **🏠 126 Rue de l'Université 75007** **Ⓜ Assemblée Nationale** **🚆 Invalides** **🌐 assemblee-nationale.fr**

Built in 1722 for the Duchesse de Bourbon, daughter of Louis XIV, the Palais-Bourbon was confiscated during the Revolution. It has been home to the lower house

of the French Parliament since 1830. During World War II, the palace became the Nazi administration's seat of government. The grand Neo-Classical façade with its fine columns was added in 1806, partly to mirror the façade of La Madeleine church facing it across the Seine. The adjacent Hôtel de Lassay is the residence of the president of the National Assembly. Group tours can be organized for a maximum of 50 people on the invitation of a member of parliament, with several months' prior notice.

Parc Rives de Seine

📍D6 🏛Quai d'Orsay 75007, Quai des Tuileries 75001 Ⓜ Assemblée Nationale, Invalides

Once a busy roadway, this pedestrianized riverside promenade is one of Paris's loveliest walks, extending 7 km (4 miles) along the Left and Right Banks and offering spectacular views of the Louvre, Jardin des Tuileries and other monuments.

Listed as a UNESCO World Heritage Site, Parc Rives de Seine makes it possible to walk, jog or cycle from the Place de la Bastille to the Eiffel Tower via various bridges. Activities for children include mini playgrounds, and climbing walls while the promenade has *pétanque* courts, a fitness course and a floating art exhibition centre, Fluctuart. There are around 15 cafés and restaurants both on land and aboard boats, especially around Pont Alexandre III. Picnickers and evening revellers gather on the banks during the summer creating a fun, festive atmosphere.

Musée de l'Ordre de la Libération

📍E7 🏛Hôtel des Invalides, 129 Rue de Grenelle/Place Vauban 75007 Ⓜ La Tour-Maubourg 🅁🅴🅁 Invalides 🕐10am-6pm daily 🚫1 Jan, 1 May, 25 Dec 🌐ordre delaliberation.fr

This museum is devoted to the wartime Free French and their leader, General Charles de Gaulle, as well as to the Resistance movement within France and the Resistance fighters who were captured and deported.

The Order of Liberation was created by De Gaulle in 1940. It is France's highest honour and was bestowed on those who made an outstanding contribution to the final victory in World War II. Among the recipients of the honour are French civilians and members of the armed forces, plus a number of overseas leaders such as King George VI, Winston Churchill and Dwight Eisenhower.

Did You Know?

The Pont de la Concorde in front of the Assemblée Nationale was built using stone from the Bastille.

CHAMPS-ÉLYSÉES AND CHAILLOT

The world's most beautiful avenue still has a shine to it. Although its shops are mainly frequented by tourists, it's worth a visit for the iconic stores and the monumental Arc de Triomphe. Well-heeled Parisians do live nearby, but are more likely to be found at one of the museums at the Palais de Chaillot. Luxury shoppers will revel in the Avenue Montaigne and the area's palace hotels are the perfect place for a ritzy afternoon tea or evening cocktail.

↓ The historic Avenue des Champs-Élysées

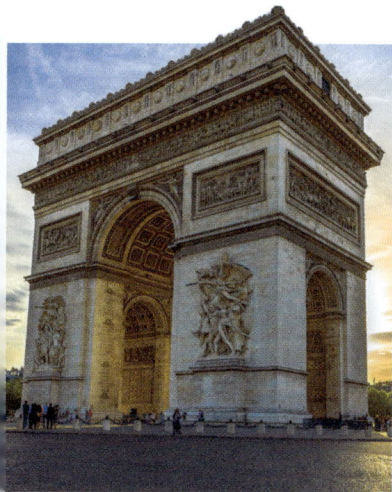

← The golden tones of the arch's stonework, highlighted by the sunset

ARC DE TRIOMPHE

📍C4 🏛Pl Charles de Gaulle Ⓜ/🚉Charles de Gaulle-Étoile 🚌22, 30, 31, 52, 73, 92 to Pl Charles de Gaulle ⏰10am–10:30pm daily (Apr–Sep: to 11pm) 🕐am only 8 May, 14 Jul, 11 Nov; all day 1 Jan, 1 May, 25 Dec 🌐paris-arc-de-triomphe.fr

Situated at the heart of Place Charles de Gaulle, overlooking the Champs-Élysées, the Arc de Triomphe was commissioned by Napoleon to celebrate France's military might. The exterior is adorned with sculptures depicting various battles, while the viewing platform at the top affords one of the best views in Paris.

After his greatest victory, the Battle of Austerlitz in 1805, Napoleon promised his men, "You shall go home beneath triumphal arches." The first stone of what was to become the world's most famous triumphal arch was laid the following year, but disruptions to architect Jean Chalgrin's plans and the demise of Napoleonic power delayed the completion of this monumental building until 1836. Standing 50 m (164 ft) high, the Arc is now the customary starting point for victory celebrations and parades.

PALAIS DE CHAILLOT

📍 B6 🏠 Pl du Trocadéro 75016 Ⓜ Trocadéro

The Palais, with its huge, curved colonnaded wings each culminating in an immense pavilion, was designed in Neo-Classical style for the 1937 World Fair (Exposition Universelle) by Léon Azéma, Louis-Hippolyte Boileau and Jacques Carlu. Today it houses three major museums: the Cité de l'Architecture et du Patrimoine, the Musée de l'Homme and the Musée National de la Marine.

The present Palais replaced the Trocadéro palace built for the World Fair of 1878. It is adorned with sculptures and bas-reliefs, and on the walls of the pavilions are gold inscriptions by the poet and essayist Paul Valéry. The *parvis*, or square, situated between the two pavilions is decorated with large bronze sculptures and ornamental pools. On the terrace in front of the *parvis* stand two bronzes, *Apollo* by Henri Bouchard and *Hercules* by Albert Pommier. Stairways lead from the terrace to the Théâtre National de Chaillot, which, since World War II, has enjoyed huge fame for its avant-garde productions.

THÉÂTRE NATIONAL DE CHAILLOT

In addition to being a prestigious performance venue, the Théâtre National de Chaillot has also played an important role in world history. It was here that the Universal Declaration of Human Rights was signed in 1948.

View of the Palais de Chaillot from ↓ the Eiffel Tower

EXPERIENCE MORE

Musée de l'Homme

📍 A6 🏛 Palais de Chaillot, Pl du Trocadéro 75016 Ⓜ Trocadéro 🕐 11am–7pm Wed-Mon 🚫 1 Jan, 1 May, 14 Jul, 25 Dec 🌐 museedel homme.fr

Situated in the west wing of the Chaillot palace, this museum traces human evolution, from prehistoric times to the present using anthropological exhibits from around the world.

It houses one of the world's most comprehensive prehistoric collections. Displays show how humans have adapted to the environment. There is also a focus on the development of language and culture.

Place Charles de Gaulle (l'Étoile)

📍 C4 🏛 75008 Ⓜ Charles de Gaulle-Étoile

Known as the Place de l'Étoile until the death of Charles de Gaulle in 1969, this roundabout, with

12 avenues radiating off it, is referred to simply as l'Étoile, "the star". As part of the revamp of the Champs-Elysées area, work is underway to reduce the space for traffic and allow more room for pedestrians to walk around the Arc de Triomphe.

Jardins du Trocadéro

📍 B6 🏛 75016 Ⓜ Trocadéro

These charming gardens were created for the 1937 Exposition Universelle. Their centrepiece is a long rectangular ornamental pool, bordered by stone and bronze-gilt statues, which look spectacular at night when the fountains are illuminated. The statues include *Man* by Pierre Traverse and *Woman* by Georges Braque, *Bull* by Paul Jouve and *Horse* by Georges Guyot. On either side of the pool, the slopes of the Chaillot hill lead down to the Seine and the Pont d'Iéna. The 10-ha (25-acre) park is laid out with flowering trees, small streams and bridges, and is a romantic place for a stroll.

> 📷 PICTURE PERFECT
> **Eiffel Tower**
>
> The palace's terrace offers magnificent views of the Eiffel Tower. Head here to get a panoramic shot of the Iron Lady.

→

The Eiffel Tower seen from the Jardins du Trocadéro

Petit Palais

📍 E5 🏠 Ave Winston Churchill 75008 Ⓜ Champs-Élysées-Clemenceau ⏰ 10am-6pm Tue-Sun (to 8pm Fri & Sat for temporary exhibitions) ❌ Public hols 🌐 petitpalais.paris.fr

Built for the Exposition Universelle in 1900, this jewel of a building now houses the Musée des Beaux-Arts de la Ville de Paris. Arranged around a pretty courtyard, the palace is similar in style to the Grand Palais, and is graced with Ionic columns, a grand porch and a dome. The wing nearest the river is used for temporary exhibitions, while the Champs-Élysées side of the palace houses the permanent collections: Greek and Roman artifacts; medieval and Renaissance ivories and sculptures; Renaissance clocks and jewellery; and 17th-, 18th-, and 19th-century art and furniture. There are also many works by the Impressionists artists.

Grand Palais

📍 E5 🏠 Porte A, Ave Général Eisenhower 75008 Ⓜ Champs-Élysées-Clemenceau 🕐 Temporarily, check website 🌐 grandpalais.fr

Built at the same time as the Petit Palais and the Pont Alexandre III,

the exterior of this massive palace combines an imposing classical stone façade with a riot of Art Nouveau ironwork. The enormous glass roof (15,000 sq m/160,000 sq ft) has Récipon's colossal bronze statues of flying horses and chariots at its four corners. The metal structure supporting the glass weighs 8,500 tonnes, some 500 tonnes more than the Eiffel Tower's.

Today, the restored Grand Palais hosts art exhibitions and other events. During the winter, the nave turns into the world's biggest indoor ice rink. Major temporary and touring exhibitions are held at the Galeries Nationales in the same building; these are often very popular and it's worth booking ahead. Check the website for details of what's on.

Avenue des Champs-Élysées

📍 D4 🏠 75008 Ⓜ Franklin D Roosevelt, George V

Paris's most famous and popular thoroughfare had its beginnings in about 1667, when the royal landscape garden designer André Le Nôtre extended the royal view from the Tuileries by creating a tree-lined avenue which eventually

became known as the Champs-Élysées (Elysian Fields). It has been France's national "triumphal way" ever since the homecoming of Napoleon's body from St Helena in 1840.

With the addition of numerous cafés and restaurants in the second half of the 19th century, the Champs-Élysées became the place in which to see and be seen. The Rond-Point des Champs-Élysées is the prettiest part, with chestnut trees and flower beds.

A number of major brands, such as H&M and Abercrombie & Fitch, have their flagship stores here, while fast-food cafés jostle for space with more upmarket establishments such as Fouquet's Brasserie

In July, the avenue is the setting for the exhilarating sprint finish of the annual Tour de France cycle race.

The Neo-Classical
entrance to the
Petit Palais

Place de la Concorde

📍F5 🏠75008
Ⓜ Concorde

One of Europe's most
magnificent and historic
squares, Place de la
Concorde covers more than
8 ha (20 acres) in the middle
of Paris. Starting out as
Place Louis XV, displaying a
statue of the eponymous
king, it was built in the mid-
18th century by architect
Jacques-Ange Gabriel, who
chose to make it an open
octagon with only the north
side containing mansions.
In the square's next incar-
nation, as the Place de la
Révolution, the statue was
replaced by the guillotine.
The death toll in the square
in two and a half years was
1,119, and victims included
Louis XVI, Marie-Antoinette
who died in view of the
secret apartment she kept
at No 2 Rue Royale) and
the Revolutionary leaders
Danton and Robespierre. In
the spirit of reconciliation,
the square was then renamed
Concorde (originally by
chastened Revolutionaries).
Its grandeur was enhanced
in the 19th century by the
arrival of the 3,200-year-old
Luxor obelisk – a gift from
Egypt, 23-m (75-ft) tall and
covered in hieroglyphics – as

well as two fountains and
eight statues personifying
French cities. It has become
the culminating point of
triumphal parades down
the Champs-Élysées each
14 July, most notably on the
memorable Bastille Day of
1989 when the Revolution's
bicentenary was celebrated
by a million people, including many world leaders.

Aquarium de Paris

📍B6 🏠5 Ave Albert de
Mun 75016 Ⓜ Trocadéro,
Iéna ⏰10am–6pm daily
(to 9pm Sat); advance
booking required 🗓14 Jul
🌐aquariumdeparis.com

Originally built in 1878 for
the Exposition Universelle,
this is now a state-of-the-
art aquarium which is home
to over 500 species of sea
creatures from around the
world, including seahorses,
clownfish, stonefish and
some spectacular sharks
and rays.

The building is located
in a former quarry and has
been designed to blend in
entirely with the Chaillot
hillside. Cinema screens
showing cartoons and
animal documentaries
are interspersed with the
aquariums, and there are
art exhibitions and shows
for children in the theatre.
The aquarium regularly
runs special late night
openings; check the
website for details.

EAT

Astrance

Go for broke at this
three-Michelin-star
restaurant with epic
tasting menus.

📍B5 🏠32 Rue
de Longchamp
75016 🌐astrance
paris.fr

€€€

Pierre Gagnaire

One of Paris's
best chefs wows
diners with a
contemporary
dining experience.

📍C4 🏠6 Rue Balzac
75008 🌐pierre-
gagnaire.com

€€€

Relais de
l'Entrecôte

Steak, chips
and nothing else.
It's a family favour-
ite; just go early
to queue up –
it doesn't take
long to get a table.

📍D5 🏠15 Rue
Marbeuf 75008
🌐relaisentrecote.fr

€€€

Palais de la Découverte

📍 E5 🏛 Ave Franklin D Roosevelt 75008 Ⓜ Franklin D Roosevelt 🕐 Until 2025 🌐 palais-decouverte.fr

Opened in a wing of the Grand Palais for the World Fair of 1937, this science museum is a Paris institution. Demonstrations and displays, including a planetarium, cover many subjects and explain such phenomena as electromagnetism. The Palais de la Découverte will remain closed to the public until 2025.

Pont Alexandre III

📍 E5 🏛 75008 Ⓜ Champs-Élysées-Clemenceau

This is Paris's prettiest bridge with its exuberant Art Nouveau decoration of lamps, cherubs, nymphs and winged horses at either end. It was built between 1896 and 1900, in time for the Exposition Universelle, and it was named after Tsar Alexander III of Russia, whose son Nicholas II laid the foundation stone in October 1896.

The style of the bridge reflects that of the Grand Palais, to which it leads on the Right Bank. The construction of the bridge is a marvel of 19th-century engineering, consisting of a 6-m- (18-ft-) high single-span steel arch that stretches across the Seine. The design was subject to strict controls that pre-vented the bridge from obscuring the view of the Champs-Élysées or the Dôme des Invalides so, today, you can still enjoy stunning views from here.

Avenue Montaigne

📍 D5 🏛 75008 Ⓜ Franklin D Roosevelt

In the 19th century, this avenue was famous for its dance halls and its Winter Garden, where Parisians went to hear Adolphe Sax play his newly invented saxophone. Today, it is still one of Paris's most fashionable streets, bustling with restaurants, cafés, hotels and designer boutiques. At one end lies the lovely Art Deco Théâtre de Champs-Élysées, built in 1913.

Parc Monceau

📍 D3 🏛 35 Blvd de Courcelles 75017 Ⓜ Monceau, Courcelles 🕐 7am-8pm daily (summer: to 10pm)

This green haven dates back to 1778 when the Duc de Chartres (later Duc d'Orléans) commissioned the painter-writer and amateur landscape designer Louis Carmontelle to create a magnificent garden. Also a theatre designer, Carmontelle created a "garden of dreams", a landscape full of architectural follies in imitation of English and German fashions of the time. In 1783, the Scottish landscape gardener Thomas Blaikie laid out an area of the garden in English style. The park was the scene of the first recorded parachute landing, made by André-Jacques Garnerin on 22 October 1797. Over the years, the park changed hands and in 1852 it was acquired by the state and half the land sold off for property development. The remaining land was made into public gardens. New buildings erected by Adolphe Alphand, architect of the Bois de Boulogne and the Bois de Vincennes.

The park, one of the most chic in Paris, has lost many of its early features. A *naumachia* basin – an

ornamental version of a Roman pool used for simulating naval battles – remains, flanked by Corinthian columns. Other remaining features include a Renaissance arcade, pyramids, statues, a river and the Pavillon de Chartres, a charming rotunda designed by Nicolas Ledoux which was once used as a toll-house. Just south of here is a huge red Chinese pagoda, the Maison Loo, which holds exhibitions of Asian art.

Musée d'Art Moderne de la Ville de Paris

📍 C6 🏛 11 Ave du Président-Wilson 75116 🚇 Iéna, Alma Marceau 🕐 10am–6pm Tue–Sun (to 9:30pm Thu) 🚇 Public hols 🌐 mam.paris.fr

This large lively museum houses the city of Paris's own renowned collection of modern art. It has about 10,000 works representing major 20th- and 21st-century artistic movements and artists. Established in 1961, the museum is one of two within the vast Palais de Tokyo, which was built for the 1937 World Fair.

One of the museum's highlights is Raoul Dufy's gigantic mural *The Spirit of Electricity*, which traces the history of electricity through the ages. It was designed for the Electricity Pavilion in the 1937 fair. One of the largest paintings in the world, measuring 600 sq metres (6,500 sq ft), this curved mural takes up a whole room of the museum.

Also notable are the Cubists, Amedeo Modigliani, George Rouault, Duchamp, Klein and the Fauves. This group of avant-garde artists, including Dufy and Derain, was dominated by Matisse, whose celebrated mural *La Danse* is on display here; you can see both the incomplete early version and the finished version. Entry to the permanent exhibition is free, while the frequent temporary exhibitions require a ticket.

←

The ornamental pond in the charming Parc Monceau

DRINK

Here are five of the best hotel bars for enjoying a decadent sundowner around the Champs-Élysées:

Le Bar at the Four Seasons Hotel George V
📍 C5 🏛 31 Ave George V 75008 🌐 fourseasons.com

Bar de l'Hôtel Belmont
📍 C5 🏛 30 Rue de Bassano 75116 🌐 belmont-paris-hotel.com

Le Bar Kléber at the Peninsula
📍 B4 🏛 19 Ave Kléber 75116 🌐 peninsula.com

Le Bar Botaniste at the Shangri-La
📍 B6 🏛 10 Ave d'Iéna 75116 🌐 shangri-la.com

Le Bar du Bristol
📍 E4 🏛 112 Rue du Faubourg-St-Honoré 75008 🌐 oetkercollection.com

ST-GERMAIN-DES-PRÉS

Cafés line the streets and squares of this iconic district – the chocolates and pastries are some of the city's best. Shoppers delight in the boutiques and art galleries found here – Le Bon Marché in particular captivates shoppers who walk through its perfume-laden halls. A smattering of museums and centuries-old churches attract tourists, but locals continue to lay claim to this bohemian enclave. There's no better place to rub elbows with Parisians than in one of the neighbourhood's plentiful cafés and bars.

Les Deux Magots, on the pleasant Boulevard St-Germain

MUSÉE D'ORSAY

📍G6 🏠1 Rue de la Légion d'Honneur Ⓜ️Solférino 🚌68, 69, 87 to Quai A France; 73 to Rue Solférino; 63, 83, 84, 94 to Blvd St-Germain 🚆Musée d'Orsay 🕐9:30am–6pm Tue-Sun (to 9:45pm Thu) 📅1 May, 25 Dec 🌐musee-orsay.fr

The Musée d'Orsay picks up where the Louvre ends, showing a variety of art forms from 1848 to 1914. Its star attraction is a superb collection of Impressionist art, which includes famous works by Monet, Renoir, Manet and Degas, as well as pieces by Georges Seurat, Gauguin and Van Gogh.

GREAT VIEW
City Panorama

Make your way to the rear escalator, ride it all the way up, and head to the small rooftop terrace for a great bird's-eye view of the city.

In 1986, 47 years after it had closed as a mainline railway station, Victor Laloux's superb late-19th-century building was reopened as the Musée d'Orsay. Originally commissioned by the Orléans railway company to be its Paris terminus, the structure avoided demolition in the 1970s after being classified as a historical monument. During the conversion into a museum, much of the original architecture was retained. The collection was set up to present each of the arts of the period from 1848 to 1914 in the context of contemporary society and other forms of creative activity happening at the time. The displays are constantly evolving, and American collectors made large donations of works in 2016 and 2019.

GALLERY GUIDE

The Musée d'Orsay's fine collection occupies three levels. The ground floor, with sculptures down the central aisle, houses Academic, Realist and Symbolist works. Temporary exhibits can be found on the middle level, along with displays on the Art Nouveau and Naturalism movements. The upper level showcases an outstanding array of Impressionist and Post-Impressionist art.

↑ The light and spacious entrance hall, with curved glass ceiling

EXPERIENCE MORE

Musée de la Légion d'Honneur

📍 G6 🏠 2 Rue de la Légion d'Honneur (Parvis du Musée d'Orsay) 75007 Ⓜ Solférino 🚇 Musée d'Orsay 🕐 1–6pm Wed–Sun 🗓 1 Jan, 1 May, 15 Aug, 1 Nov, 24 & 25 Dec 🌐 legiondhonneur.fr

Next to the Musée d'Orsay is the truly massive Hôtel de Salm. It was one of the last great mansions to be built in the area (1782). The first owner was a German count, Prince de Salm-Kyrbourg, who was guillotined in 1794.

Today, the building contains a museum where you can learn all about the Legion of Honour, a decoration launched by Napoleon I. Those awarded the honour wear a small red rosette in their buttonhole. The impressive displays of medals and insignia are complemented by paintings. In one of the rooms, Napoleon's Legion of Honour is on display with his sword and breastplate.

The museum also contains examples of decorations from most parts of the world, among them the British Victoria Cross and the American Purple Heart.

Académie Française

📍 H7 🏠 23 Quai de Conti 75006 Ⓜ Pont Neuf, St-Germain-des-Prés 🌐 academie-francaise.fr

This striking Baroque edifice was built as a school for young noblemen in 1688 and given over to the Institut de France in 1805. Its cupola was designed by architect Louis Le Vau to harmonize with the Palais du Louvre.

The Académie Française is the oldest of the five academies of the institute. Founded in 1635 by Cardinal Richelieu, it is charged with regulating the French language by deciding acceptable grammar and vocabulary, and with the compilation of an official dictionary of the French language. From the beginning, membership has been limited to 40 scholars, who are entrusted with a lifelong commitment to working on the dictionary. The building is only open to the public during the Journées du Patrimoine (Heritage Days) on the third weekend of September.

Musée Eugène Delacroix

📍 H7 📍 6 Rue de Fürstenberg 75006 Ⓜ St-Germain-des-Prés, Mabillon 🕐 9:30am–5:30pm Wed-Mon; advance booking recommended 🗓 1 Jan, 1 May, 25 Dec 🌐 musee-delacroix.fr

The leading nonconformist Romantic painter Eugène Delacroix, known for his passionate and highly coloured canvases, lived and worked here from 1857 to his death in 1863. Here, he painted *The Entombment of Christ* and *The Way to Calvary* (which now hang in the museum). He also created superb murals for the Chapel of the Holy Angels in the nearby St-Sulpice church, which is part of the reason why he moved to this area. The first-floor apartment

←

The Académie Française, ultimate arbiter of French language and grammar

and garden studio now form a national museum, where regular exhibitions of Delacroix's work are held. The apartment has portraits, studies for future works and artistic memorabilia.

The charm of Delacroix's garden is reflected in the tiny Fürstenberg square. With its pair of rare catalpa trees and old-fashioned street lamps, the square is one of Paris's most romantic corners.

St-Germain-des-Prés

📍 H7 📍 3 Pl St-Germain-des-Prés 75006 Ⓜ St-Germain-des-Prés 🕐 9:30am–8pm Sun & Mon, 8:30am–8pm Tue-Sat 🌐 eglise-saint germaindespres.fr

This is the oldest church in Paris, originating in 543 when King Childebert built a basilica to house holy relics. It became a powerful Benedictine abbey, which was suppressed during the French Revolution, when most of the buildings were destroyed by a fire.

The present church dates from about the 11th century and was restored in the 19th century. The interior is a mix of architectural styles, with 6th-century marble columns, Gothic vaulting and Romanesque arches. Famous tombs include that of René Descartes.

Café de Flore

📍 H7 📍 172 Blvd St-Germain 75006 Ⓜ St-Germain-des-Prés 🕐 7:30am–1:30am daily 🌐 cafedeflore.fr

The classic Art Deco interior of this café has changed little since World War II. Like its neighbouring rival Les Deux Magots, Café de Flore has hosted most of the French intellectuals during the post-War years.

École Nationale Supérieure des Beaux-Arts

📍 H7 📍 13 Quai Malaquais & 14 Rue Bonaparte 75006 Ⓜ St-Germain-des-Prés 🌐 beauxartsparis.fr

The main French school of fine arts occupies an enviable position at the corner of Rue Bonaparte and the riverside Quai Malaquais. The school is housed in several buildings, the most imposing being the 19th-century Palais des Études. A host of budding French and foreign painters and architects have crossed the large courtyard to study in the ateliers of the school. Young American architects, in particular, have frequented the halls since the late 19th century. Works from its collections can be viewed in regular exhibitions.

Monnaie de Paris

📍H7 🏛11 Quai de Conti 75006 Ⓜ Pont Neuf, Odéon 🕐11am–6pm Tue–Sun (to 9pm Wed) 🚫1 Jan, 1 May, 25 Dec ⓦmonnaiedeparis.fr

In the late 18th century, when Louis XV decided to rehouse the Mint, he launched a design competition for the new building. The Hôtel des Monnaies is the result. It was completed in 1775, and the architect, Jacques Antoine, lived here until his death.

Coins were minted in the mansion until 1973, when the process was moved to Pessac in the Gironde. The whole complex can now be visited, including its interior courtyards, garden and museum, the Musée de la Monnaie de Paris. Centred around a tranquil public

space and surrounded by artists' workshops, the permanent gallery focuses on the history of coins and minting. Regular exhibitions of contemporary art are also staged here, as well as workshops for both families and adults, such as making coins out of chocolate. There are also shops selling work by resident artisans, a gastronomic restaurant run by chef Guy Savoy and a more casual café.

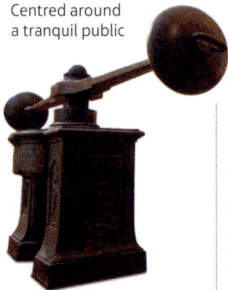

↑ A coin press at the newly revamped Monnaie de Paris

Rue St-André-des-Arts

📍J8 🏛75006 Ⓜ St-Michel, Odéon

Extending from Place St-André-des-Arts, where the square's namesake church once stood, this little street features a number of historical monuments.

Dating back to 1179, Rue St-André-des-Arts once led to the gate of the city in the former Philippe Auguste wall. The sumptuous mansion at No 27 was owned by Louis XIII's geographer in the 1600s, while renowned grammarian and encyclopaedist Pierre Larousse lived at No 49 in the 19th century. Peeling south off Rue St-André-des-Arts is the cobbled Cour du Commerce, home to many shops and restaurants.

Cour du Commerce St-André

📍J8 🏛75006 Ⓜ Odéon

No 9 in this historic passage has a particularly grisly past, because it was here that Dr Guillotin is supposed to have perfected his "philanthropic decapitating machine". In fact, although the idea was Guillotin's, it was Dr Antoine Louis, a Parisian surgeon, who was responsible for putting the "humane" plan into action. When the guillotine was first used for execution in 1792, it was known as a *Louisette*.

Le Procope

📍J8 🏛13 Rue de l'Ancienne-Comédie 75006 Ⓜ Odéon 🕐Noon–midnight daily (to 1am Thu–Sat) ⓦprocope.com

Founded in 1686 by the Sicilian Francesco Procopio dei Coltelli, this claims to be the world's first coffee house. It quickly became popular with the city's political and cultural elite. Its illustrious patrons have included the philosopher Voltaire – who supposedly drank 40 cups of his favourite mixture of coffee and chocolate every day – and the young Napoleon, who would leave his hat as security while he went searching for the money to pay the bill. Le Procope is now an 18th-century-style restaurant serving *coq au vin* and other brasserie classics.

St-Sulpice

Q H8 **⌂** 2 Rue Palatine, Pl St-Sulpice 75006 **M** St-Sulpice **🕒** 8am-7:45pm daily **W** paroisse saintsulpice.paris

It took over a century, from 1646, for this imposing church to be built. The result is a simple two-storey west front with two tiers of elegant columns. The overall harmony of the building is marred only by the towers, one at each end, which do not match.

Large arched windows fill the interior with light. By the front door are two huge shells given to François I by the Venetian Republic – they rest on bases sculpted by Jean-Baptiste Pigalle.

In the side chapel to the right of the main door are three magnificent murals by Eugène Delacroix: *Jacob Wrestling with the Angel*, *Heliodorus Driven from the Temple* and *St Michael Killing*

the Dragon. If you are lucky, you can catch an organ recital. Regular guided tours of the church take place at 2:30pm every Sunday.

Le Bon Marché

Q G8 **⌂** 24 Rue de Sèvres 75007 **M** Sèvres-Babylone **🕒** 10am-7:45pm Mon-Sat, 11am-7:45pm Sun **W** lebon marche.com

Welcoming as many as 15,000 customers per day, "The Good Market" (or "The Good Deal") is the swankiest department store in Paris, selling luxury goods and gourmet foods in its annexe La Grande Épicerie at No 38 Rue du Bac. The designer clothing section is well sourced, the high-end accessories are excellent, and the own-brand linen has a good quality-to-price ratio.

Le Bon Marché is also the world's oldest department store, founded in 1852 by Aristide Boucicaut and his wife. The Boucicauts used their keen sense of commerce to introduce innovative practices – fixed prices, sales, home delivery, advertising and guarantees – that became the standard for other *grands magasins*. Designed by Louis-Charles Boileau and Gustave Eiffel, it is an architectural landmark.

EAT

Semilla

Sharing plates and fresh, innovative cooking with local ingredients are on the menu here.

Q H7 **⌂** 54 Rue de Seine 75006 **W** semillaparis.com

€€€

Le Comptoir du Relais

This bistro is a staple of the area for inventive French cooking at lunch and dinner.

Q H8 **⌂** 9 Carrefour de l'Odéon 75006 **W** hotel-paris-relais-saint-germain.com

€€€

Ze Kitchen Galerie

French cooking is infused with international inspirations at this one-Michelin-star restaurant.

Q J7 **⌂** 4 Rue des Grands Augustins 75006 **🕒** Sat, Sun **W** zekitchengalerie.fr

€€€

Pont des Arts

📍H7 🏠75006

Ⓜ Louvre-Rivoli

Sometimes referred to as the Passerelle des Arts, this picturesque iron bridge, part of the UNESCO-listed Parisian riverfront, has more often been called the "Love Lock Bridge" in recent years. The popular nickname refers to the now-forbidden practice of couples fixing padlocks to the bridge to signify their love; the practice had to be stopped because the locks exerted too much weight on the structure and started to destroy it.

Now revived and restored – following the removal of almost a million locks weighing 45 tonnes – this pedestrian bridge, built under Napoleon from 1801 to 1804, has been returned to its 19th-century splendour. The first iron bridge in Paris, it links the Institut de France with the Louvre, offering resplendent views of the Île de la Cité from above the river. At night, illuminated every so often by the Bateaux Mouches cruising gently underneath, the Pont des Arts is an especially romantic place to walk or picnic in warmer months.

Deyrolle

📍G7 🏠46 Rue du Bac 75005 Ⓜ Rue du Bac

🕐10am–7pm Mon–Sat

🅦 deyrolle.com

A Parisian institution since 1831 and beloved by artists like Salvador Dalí,

THE CELEBRATED CAFÉS OF PARIS

One of the most enduring images of Paris is the café scene. For the visitor, it is the romantic vision of great artists, writers or eminent intellectuals consorting in one of the Left Bank's celebrated cafés. For the Parisian, the café is one of life's constants, an every day experience, providing people with a place to tryst, drink and meet friends, to conclude business deals, or to simply watch the world go by.

The most famous cafés are on the Left Bank, in St-Germain and Montparnasse. Sartre and his intellectual peers, among them the writers Simone de Beauvoir and Albert Camus, gathered to work and discuss their ideas in Les Deux Magots and Café de Flore.

← The Pont des Arts with its prime views of the Île de la Cité

Deyrolle is a cabinet of curiosities that continues to delight all who enter its doors. Originally a taxidermy shop, it has evolved over the years, and now part of its mission is to raise awareness about wildlife conservation. The casual visitor, however, can simply enjoy the collection of taxidermied animals, from giant elephants and rhinos to the most delicate birds and crustaceans. There is a wide range of insects housed in drawers. Iridescent beetles and colourful butterflies sit alongside terrifying tarantulas and scorpions. Everything is for sale, mostly at decent prices considering the quality.

Musée Maillol

9 G7 **⌂** 59/61 Rue de Grenelle 75007 **M** Sèvres-Babylone, Rue du Bac **⏱** 10:30am–6:30pm daily (to 10pm Wed) **🗓** 1 Jan, 25 Dec **w** museemaillol.com

Once the home of novelist Alfred de Musset, this museum was created by Dina Vierny, former model of Aristide Maillol in an 18th-century building that used to be a convent.

All aspects of the artist's work are here: drawings, engravings, paintings, sculpture and decorative objects. Also displayed is Vierny's private collection, including works by Matisse, Picasso and Rodin.

The museum stages regular temporary art exhibitions, which are usually based on themes and artists associated with Maillol.

Large allegorical figures of the city of Paris, the River Seine and the four seasons decorate Edme Bouchardon's fountain, *La Fontaine des Quatre Saisons*, built in 1739–45, in front of the house.

Les Deux Magots

9 H7 **⌂** 6 Pl St-Germain-des-Prés 75006 **M** St-Germain-des-Prés **⏱** 7:30am–1am daily **🗓** One week in Jan **w** lesdeuxmagots.com

Established in 1914, this charming café still trades on its reputation as the meeting place of the city's literary and intellectual elite. This derives from the patron-age of Surrealist artists and writers, including Ernest Hemingway, in the 1920s and 1930s, and existentialist philosophers and writers in the 1950s. The present clientele, however, is more likely to consist

TOP 5 SHOPPING STREETS

Rue Lobineau
9 H8
Home of the St-Germain food market.

Rue Bonaparte
9 H8
Full of swanky shops, including the Pierre Hermé flagship.

Rue du Bac
9 G7
Full of pastry shops and other confections.

Rue de Sèvres
9 G8
The location of Le Bon Marché, Paris's first department store.

Rue de Buci
9 H8
A former market street that now houses cafés and appealing shops.

of publishers or people-watchers than the new Hemingway.

The name of the café comes from the two wooden statues of Chinese *magots* (commercial agents) that adorn one of the pillars. This is a good place for enjoying an old-fashioned hot chocolate or a classic French omelette and watching the world go by from a seat on the wraparound terrace.

LATIN QUARTER

From Romans ruins to Hollywood backdrops, the Latin Quarter is beloved by Parisians and travellers alike. Café crowds are decidedly younger than most, filled with university students from the Collège de France and La Sorbonne. Every block seems to have a bookstore, from obscure academic shops to the bursting shelves of the famed Shakespeare and Company. Peppered along the tiny twisting streets are crêpe stands and dive bars, all offset by the grandeur of stunning sights such as the Panthéon, Musée de Cluny and Church of St-Étienne-du-Mont.

↓ The Shakespeare and Company bookshop

PANTHÉON

📍 J9 🏛 Pl du Panthéon Ⓜ Cardinal Lemoine, Maubert-Mutualité 🚌 84 to Panthéon; 21, 27, 38, 82, 85, 89 to Gare du Luxembourg 🚆 Luxembourg 🕐 10am-6:30pm daily (Oct-Mar: to 6pm); dome: Apr-Oct 🚫 1 Jan, 1 May, 25 Dec 🌐 paris-pantheon.fr

Inspired by the Pantheon in Rome, Paris's Panthéon was originally built as a church. Today a public building, it provides a fitting final resting place for the nation's great figures.

When Louis XV recovered from desperate illness in 1744, he was so grateful to be alive that he conceived a magnificent church to honour Sainte Geneviève. The design was entrusted to the French architect Jacques-Germain Soufflot, who planned the church in Neo-Classical style. Work began in 1757 and was completed in 1790, ten years after Soufflot's death, under the supervision of Guillaume Rondelet. But with the Revolution under way, the church was soon turned into a pantheon – a location for the tombs of France's great and good. Napoleon returned it to the Church in 1806, but it was secularized and then desecularized once more before finally being made a civic building in 1885.

Did You Know?

The dome was inspired by St Paul's in London and the Dôme des Invalides.

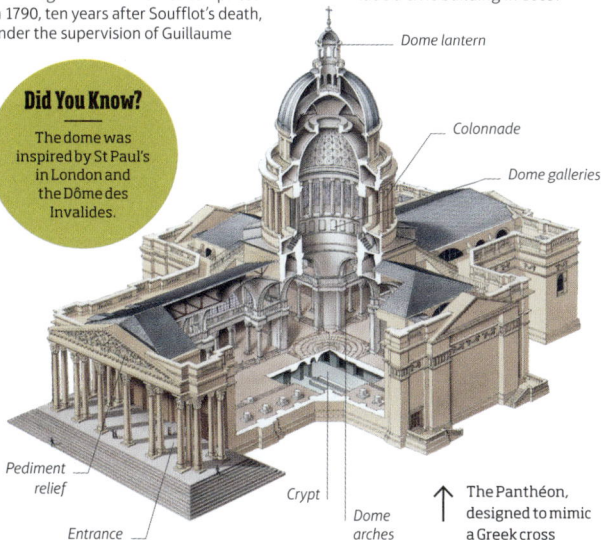

Dome lantern

Colonnade

Dome galleries

Pediment relief

Crypt

Dome arches

Entrance

↑ The Panthéon, designed to mimic a Greek cross

EXPERIENCE MORE

The chapel of La Sorbonne, with its elegant dome

Shakespeare and Company

⊙ K8 ⌂ 37 Rue de la Bûcherie 75005 ⊙ 10am–8pm Mon–Sat, noon–7pm Sun Ⓜ St-Michel, Maubert-Mutualité Ⓦ shakespeareand company.com

George Whitman opened this now-iconic shop in 1951. Originally called Le Mistral, it was renamed Shakespeare and Company in 1964 after the renowned bookshop run by Sylvia Beach on nearby Rue de l'Odéon, which closed in 1941 during the Occupation. Whitman sought to emulate the spirit of Beach's shop, attracting expat writers like Henry Miller and Anaïs Nin. Over the years, the owner allowed young writers to sleep in the shop for free, asking them only to read, help at the shop and write a page-long autobiography. The shop continues Whitman's traditions, under his daughter Sylvia – named after Beach.

There are always literary events taking place here, some featuring big names such as David Sedaris, Zadie Smith and Carol Ann Duffy. Although the shop is tiny, it is well stocked with contemporary literature, Paris-themed books and English travel books.

Right next door is a coffee shop, where you can settle down with a book at one of the outdoor tables facing Notre-Dame.

St-Séverin

⊙ J8 ⌂ 3 Rue des Prêtres-St-Séverin 75005 Ⓜ St-Michel ⊙ 9:30am–1pm & 2–7:30pm Mon–Sat, 9am–1pm & 3–8pm Sun Ⓦ saint-severin.com

One of the most beautiful churches in Paris and a popular venue for concerts, St-Séverin, named after a 6th-century hermit who lived in the area, is a perfect example of the Flamboyant Gothic style. Construction finished during the early 16th century and included a remarkable double ambulatory circling the chancel.

In 1684, the Grande Mademoiselle, cousin to Louis XIV, adopted the church after breaking with St-Sulpice and had its chancel modernized.

Collège de France

⊙ J9 ⌂ 11 Pl Marcelin-Berthelot 75005 Ⓜ Maubert-Mutualité ⊙ Sep–Jun: 10am–6pm Mon–Fri ⌂ School hols Ⓦ college-de-france.fr

One of Paris's esteemed institutes of research and learning, the college was established in 1530 by François I. Guided by the great humanist Guillaume Budé, the king aimed to counteract the rigidity and traditionalism of the Sorbonne. A statue of Budé stands in the west courtyard, and the unbiased approach to learning is reflected in the inscription on the old college entrance: *docet omnia* (all are taught here). Lectures are free and open to the public, see the website for details.

La Sorbonne

⊙ J9 ⌂ 1 Rue Victor Cousin 75005 Ⓜ Cluny-La Sorbonne, Odéon Ⓦ sorbonne-universite.fr

The Sorbonne, seat of the University of Paris, was

Ⓠ HIDDEN GEM
Thermes de Cluny

These Roman baths were built at the end of the 1st century CE. In the 14th century the Cluny monks built their abbey over the ruins and today they can be seen as part of a visit to the Musée de Cluny.

established in 1253 by Robert de Sorbon, confessor to Louis IX, for 16 underprivileged students to study theology. Within a few years, the college became the centre of scholastic theology in Paris. In 1469, the rector had three printing machines brought over from Mainz, thereby founding the first printing house in France. The college's opposition to liberal 18th-century philosophy led to its suppression during the Revolution.

In 1806, La Sorbonne was re-established by Napoleon. The buildings built by Richelieu in the early 17th century were replaced by the ones seen today, with the exception of the chapel. You can book onto a guided tour by emailing ahead.

Bibliothèque Ste-Geneviève

🚇 J9 🏠 10 Place du Panthéon 75005 Ⓜ Maubert-Mutualité ⏰ 10am–10pm Mon–Sat; tours: hours vary Wed & Sat, advance booking required Ⓦ bsg.univ-paris3.fr

This massive, sober-looking library houses some two million documents salvaged from the nearby abbey of Ste-Geneviève. Visitors to the neighbourhood may completely overlook it, as the enormous dome of the Panthéon tends to command more attention. It was, however, the first French library that was built without any connection to a palace or school building. It opened to the public in 1851, and architect Henri Labrouste

EAT

Shakespeare and Co Café

Sip coffee and nibble cakes outside the iconic bookshop.

🚇 K8 🏠 37 Rue de la Bûcherie 75005 Ⓦ shakespeareandcompany.com

€€€

Chez Gladines

Hearty and affordable no-frills French meals.

🚇 K8 🏠 44 Blvd St-Germain 75005 Ⓦ chezgladines-saintgermain.fr

€€€

La Tour d'Argent

Try the legendary duck at this historic restaurant that was much loved by Henri IV.

🚇 L8 🏠 17 Quai de la Tournelle 75005 🔒 Sun, Mon Ⓦ tourdargent.com

€€€

incorporated a soaring glass-and-iron ceiling into the main reading room.

Square René Viviani

K8 **25 Quai de Montebello 75005**
St-Michel, Maubert-Mutualité **8am-5pm Mon-Fri, 9am-5pm Sat & Sun (summer: to 8:30pm daily)**

One of many little green oases in Paris, Square René Viviani has views of Notre-Dame that beat all others. The park was once a graveyard belonging to the 6th-century basilica that formerly stood here. Now, the church St-Julien-le-Pauvre, begun in the 12th century, sits adjacent to the park. Its most notable feature is a black locust tree (Robinia pseudoacacia), allegedly planted in 1601. Held up by a couple of concrete stilts, it is generally accepted to be the oldest tree in Paris, having survived shell damage during World War I.

The square owes its name to France's first Labour Minister, René Viviani, who once spoke out in support of women's suffrage – albeit, in a limited fashion.

Place St-Michel

J8 **75005**
St-Michel

This square at a busy intersection is a popular meeting place for Parisians and tour groups. Created in 1855, it's defined by the statue of Saint Michael the archangel slaying Satan, part of the monumental fountain built into the side of an adjacent building. The mix of colours and motifs earned it some criticism initially, and it was the last monumental wall fountain to be built in the city, ending the Renaissance-era trend brought to Paris by Catherine de Medici. Originally the fountain was meant to honour Napoleon Bonaparte, but the city council thought better of it and opted not to ruffle the feathers of anti-Bonaparte reactionaries. Nowadays, the fountain is a memorable welcome to the Latin Quarter for visitors entering the district from Île St-Louis. It is surrounded by cafés and bookshops which are popular with local university students.

St-Étienne-du-Mont

K9 **30 Rue Descartes, Pl Ste-Geneviève 75005**
Cardinal Lemoine **Hours vary, check website** **saintetienne dumont.fr**

This remarkable church houses the shrine of Sainte Geneviève, patron saint of Paris, as well as the remains of the great literary figures Racine and Pascal. Some parts are in the Gothic style and others date from the Renaissance, including a magnificent rood screen that crosses the nave like a bridge. The stained-glass windows are also of note.

Marché Maubert

K8 **Place Maubert 75005** **7am-2:30pm Tue & Thu, 7am-3pm Sat**
Maubert-Mutualité

Popular with locals, this is one of the city's oldest outdoor markets, dating

← Square René Viviani, a perfect retreat from the bustle of the city

back to 1547. In earlier times the square was a place where carriage drivers emptied their waste, creating a truly gut-wrenching stench that drove out many inhabitants. Eventually the city cleaned up the mess and repurposed the square as a place for public executions, installing breaking wheels and gibbets here in the 16th century. By the 19th century the square had returned to commercial use, and included a unique market where beggars would sell unused tobacco that they collected from the streets.

Today the market is entirely wholesome, and you can browse stalls selling local specialities such as organic strawberries, cheese and dried hams.

Grand Action Cinéma

? K9 **🏠** 5 Rue des Écoles 75005 **M** Cardinal Lemoine, Jussieu **W** legrandaction.com

Located in the heart of the Latin Quarter, this tiny independent operation is one of the most exciting cinematic experiences in Paris. The site has been a handball court, a Revolutionaries' meeting place and a dance hall over the years. Today it welcomes all sorts of films and retrospectives, ranging from niche independent films to Oscar-nominated pictures. The director and local student clubs regularly host industry professionals for talks to the public on themes such as science-fiction movies or Russian films. There are just two theatres with rows of red-cushioned seats, but the Grand Action perseveres even as multiplexes have risen in popularity.

St-Julien-le-Pauvre

? K8 **🏠** 79 Rue Galande 75005 **C** 01 43 54 52 16 **M** St-Michel **RER** St-Michel–Notre-Dame **?** 2–6:30pm daily

At least three saints can claim to be patron of this church, but the most likely is St Julian the Hospitaller. The church, together with St-Germain-des-Prés, is one of the oldest in Paris, dating from between 1165 and 1220. The university held its official meetings in the church until 1524, when a student protest created so much damage that meetings were barred from the church by parliament. Since 1889, it has belonged to the Melchite sect of the Greek Orthodox Church, and it is now the setting for chamber and religious music concerts.

DRINK

Monk le Taverne de Cluny

Craft beer has infiltrated the Parisian scene, and Monk le Taverne de Cluny is one of the best places to savour it on the Left Bank.

? J8 **🏠** 51 Rue de la Harpe 75005 **C** 01 43 54 28 88

Le Piano Vache

Students and locals hit the bar at this rowdy watering hole. Jazz concerts are held every Monday.

? K9 **🏠** 8 Rue Laplace 75005 **C** 01 46 33 75 03 **?** Sun

Le Bombardier

Paris has a few pubs worthy of the name, but this traditional British pub has earned its stripes. The draught beers are a must-try.

? K9 **🏠** 2 Place du Panthéon 75005 **W** bombardier pub.fr

JARDIN DES PLANTES AND PLACE D'ITALIE

Many people stop at the Latin Quarter, leaving this corner of the Left Bank less busy than the rest. The flowering Jardin des Plantes is home to natural history galleries and a zoo, and is a popular spot with Parisian families at weekends. A stroll along Rue Mouffetard delights with cheese and pastry shops, while architectural surprises such as the mosque or the national library make an exciting break from the traditional Parisian cityscape.

↓ A tree-lined avenue in the Jardin des Plantes

↑ The spectacular Grande Galerie de l'Évolution

MUSÉUM NATIONAL D'HISTOIRE NATURELLE

📍 L10 🏛 Grande Galerie de l'Évolution and Galerie de Géologie et de Minéralogie: 36 Rue Geoffroy St-Hilaire 75005; Galerie de Paléontologie et d'Anatomie: 2 Rue Buffon 75005 Ⓜ Jussieu, Gare d'Austerlitz 🕐 10am–6pm Wed–Mon 📅 1 Jan, 1 May, 25 Dec 🌐 mnhn.fr

This collection of galleries in the Jardin des Plantes houses an impressive display of natural history specimens tracing the evolution of life on Earth.

A botany research centre in the 17th century, the museum was founded in 1793 to include zoology. It has three galleries in the Jardin des Plantes: the Galerie de Minéralogie et de Géologie, with crystals, gems and meteorites; the Galeries d'Anatomie Comparée et de Paléontologie, housing dinosaur skeletons and fossils; and the Grande Galerie de l'Évolution, featuring stuffed tigers and elephants. The 67 million specimens here form the world's third-largest research collection. The Galerie des Enfants, in the Grande Galerie de l'Évolution, is an environment-focused exhibition for children.

The museum also encompasses several other sites in the Jardin des Plantes, including the greenhouses and the zoo.

EXPERIENCE MORE

→
St-Médard and a Rue
Mouffetard street market

Grande Mosquée de Paris

📍 L10 🏛 2 bis Pl du Puits de l'Ermite 75005 (Turkish baths/tearoom: 39 Rue Geoffroy St-Hilaire) Ⓜ Jussieu, Place Monge 🕐 9am-6pm Sat-Thu; baths: 10am-9pm daily 🌐 Muslim hols 🌐 grandemosqueede paris.fr

Built in the 1920s in the Hispano-Moorish style, this complex is the spiritual centre of Paris's Muslim community and the home of the Grand Imam. It comprises religious, educational and commercial sections; and at its heart is a mosque. Each of the mosque's domes is decorated in a different style, and the minaret stands nearly 33 m (100 ft) high. Inside is a grand patio with mosaics on the walls and tracery on the arches.

Once used only by scholars, the mosque's place in Parisian life has grown over the years. The Turkish baths are strictly for women only. A tearoom and restaurant set in a peaceful tree-shaded courtyard serve Moorish specialities and make a lovely spot for a glass of mint tea and sticky cakes.

Jardin des Plantes

📍 L9 🏛 57 Rue Cuvier 75005 Ⓜ Jussieu, Gare d'Austerlitz 🕐 Summer: 7:30am-8pm daily; winter: 8am-5:30pm daily 🌐 jardindesplantes.de paris.fr

A treasure to locals living in the 5th arrondissement, the expansive Jardin des Plantes comprises a museum, a zoo, botanical gardens, a science lab and a university research centre. Previously known as the Jardin du Roi, it started life as a medicinal herb garden created by Guy de la Brosse and Jean Hérouard, King Louis XIII's physicians, in 1626. After opening to the public in 1640 and offering a free school of botany, chemistry and anatomy, it quickly attracted renowned scientists, such as the Comte de Buffon, whose studies were to shape Darwin's views on evolution.

Today, this popular botanical garden is home to three galleries of the Muséum National d'Histoire Naturelle. It includes a small zoo, rose garden and a labyrinth that kids adore. As well as beautiful vistas and walkways flanked by ancient trees and punctuated with statues, the park features a remarkable alpine garden with plants from Himalayas, the Alps, Corsica and Morocco, and an unrivalled display of herbaceous and wild plants. It also has the first cedar of Lebanon planted in France, originally from Britain's Kew Gardens.

St-Médard

📍 K10 🏛 141 Rue Mouffetard 75005 Ⓜ Censier-Daubenton 🕐 9am-7:30pm Tue-Sat, 9am-8pm Sun 🌐 saintmedard.org

The origins of this historic church go back to as early as the 9th century. St Médard, counsellor to the Merovingian kings, was known for giving a wreath of white roses to young girls noted for their virtue. The churchyard became notorious in the 18th century as the centre of the cult of the Convulsionnaires, whose hysterical fits were brought on by the contemplation of miracle cures.

The interior features a number of beautiful paintings, including the 17th-century *St Joseph Walking with the Christ Child* by Francisco de Zurbarán. There's also an organ loft,

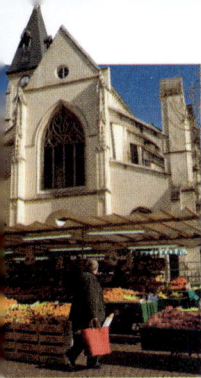

which is adorned with
Renaissance statues.

Ménagerie

L9 **57 Rue Cuvier/
Rue Buffon 75005**
**Jussieu, Gare d'
Austerlitz** **10am-
5pm daily** **jardindes
plantesdeparis.fr**

Opened in 1794, France's
oldest public zoo sits in the
pleasant surroundings of
the Jardin des Plantes. The
Ménagerie was set up
during the Revolution to
house the survivors from
the royal menagerie at
Versailles – all four of them.
The state then expanded
the collection with animals
rounded up from circuses
and creatures sent from
abroad. Tragically, during
the Prussian siege of Paris
(1870–71), most of the animals were slaughtered to
feed the hungry citizens.
The zoo specializes in
small mammals, insects,
birds, primates and reptiles.
It is a great favourite with
children as it allows them
to get quite close to the
animals, and feeding times
are especially popular.
There is an emphasis on
animals threatened with
extinction, including red
pandas, snow leopards,
Arabian oryx and Aldabra
giant tortoises. The
displays in the vivarium
(enclosures of live animals
in their natural habitat)
are changed at regular
intervals, and there is a
permanent exhibition
of microarthropods (also
known as creepy-crawlies).

Institut du
Monde Arabe

L9 **1 Rue des
Fossés St-Bernard,
Pl Mohammed V 75005**
**Jussieu, Cardinal
Lemoine** **Museum
and temporary exhibits:
10am-6pm daily (to 7pm
Sat & Sun)** **imarabe.org**

This cultural institute was
founded in 1980 by France
and 20 Arab countries
with the intention of
fostering cultural links
between the Arab world
and the West. It is
housed in a magnificent
building designed by Jean
Nouvel (who was also
responsible for the Musée
du quai Branly and the
Philharmonie), combining
modern materials with the
spirit of traditional Arab
architecture. The white
marble book tower, which
can be seen through the
glass of the west wall,
spirals upwards, bringing
to mind the minaret of a
mosque. The emphasis
that is traditionally placed
on interior space in Arab
architecture has been used
here to create an enclosed
courtyard reached by a
narrow gap splitting the
building in two.

From floors four to
seven, there's a fascinating
display of Islamic works
of art from the 9th to the
19th centuries, including
ceramics, sculpture, carpets
and astrolabes. The centre
also houses a library and
media archive, and puts
on a lively programme of
lectures and concerts.

EAT

Au P'tit Grec
A popular spot
serving huge
takeaway crêpes.

K10 **68 Rue
Mouffetard 75005**
auptitgrec.com

€ € €

MONTPARNASSE AND JARDIN DU LUXEMBOURG

Old and new Paris come together in this patch of the Left Bank, where traditional cafés nestle alongside modern tower blocks. Parisians gather alfresco in the gorgeous Jardin du Luxembourg, while in-the-know visitors head to the Tour Montparnasse and the Catacombs. Locals still congregate at the belle époque brasseries, where the appetizing smell of lentils and sausages is accompanied by the sound of clinking beers.

The Fontaine Médicis
in the Jardin du
↓ Luxembourg

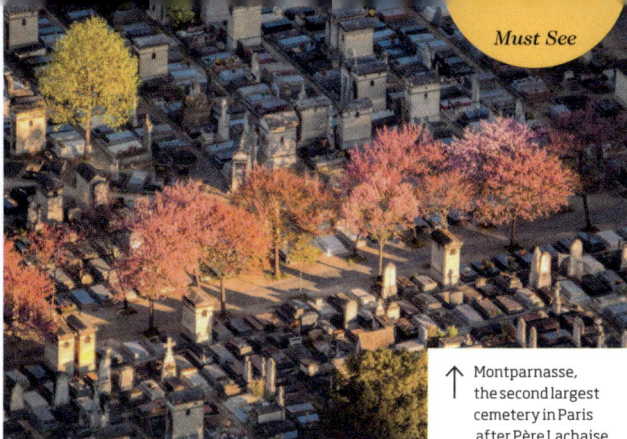

↑ Montparnasse, the second largest cemetery in Paris after Père Lachaise

CIMETIÈRE DU MONTPARNASSE

📍 G10 🏠 3 Blvd Edgar Quinet 75014 Ⓜ Edgar Quinet 🚌 28, 58, 68, 82, 83, 88, 91 to Port Royal ⓇⒺⓇ Port Royal 🕐 Mid-Mar–mid-Nov: 8am–6pm Mon–Fri, 8:30am–6pm Sat, 9am–6pm Sun (mid-Nov–mid-Mar: to 5:30pm)

This cemetery is the resting place of many illustrious Parisians. Sculptures nestle among the funerary art, creating a peaceful haven in the tree-lined grounds.

The Montparnasse Cemetery was planned by Napoleon outside the city walls to replace the numerous, congested, small cemeteries within the old city, viewed as a health hazard at the turn of the 19th century. It was opened in 1824 and contains the graves of many notable, particularly Left Bank, personalities. Like all French cemeteries, it is divided into rigidly aligned paths. The Rue Émile Richard cuts it into two parts, the Grand and the Petit Cimetière.

CHARLES BAUDELAIRE

The cemetery contains the cenotaph of Charles Baudelaire, the great poet and critic. Baudelaire, who was born and died in Paris, shocked the world with his frank and decadent collection of poems *Les Fleurs du Mal*, published in 1857. His work has had a widespread literary influence, and has even inspired rock stars such as Mick Jagger.

EXPERIENCE MORE

EXPERIENCE Montparnasse and Jardin du Luxembourg

Musée Bourdelle

📍F10 🏠18 Rue Antoine Bourdelle 75015 Ⓜ Montparnasse-Bienvenüe, Falguière ⏰10am–6pm Tue–Sun 🚫Public hols 🌐bourdelle.paris.fr

The prolific sculptor Antoine Bourdelle lived and worked in the studio here from 1884 until his death in 1929. The house, studio and garden are now a museum. Among the 900 sculptures on display are the original plaster casts of his monumental works planned for wide public squares. They also include the group of sculptures for the relief decoration of the Théâtre des Champs-Élysées. A renovation in 2022–23 has resulted in an improved permanent exhibition, and the addition of a café-restaurant overlooking the inner garden.

Musée du Luxembourg

📍H9 🏠19 Rue de Vaugirard 75006 Ⓜ St-Sulpice 🚇Luxembourg ⏰10:30am–7pm daily during exhibitions; book online 🚫1 May, 25 Dec 🌐museeduluxembourg.fr

Orginally housed in the east wing of the Palais du Luxembourg, France's first public gallery moved to this building, the palace's grand former orangery, in 1886. The collection contained works by renowned artists such as Leonardo da Vinci, Van Dyck and Rembrandt, many of which have since been moved to the Louvre. Following extensive renovations, today the museum hosts impressive temporary exhibitions on leading artists, including Rubens, Cézanne and Pissaro.

Palais du Luxembourg

📍H9 🏠19 Rue de Vaugirard 75006 Ⓜ Odéon 🚇 Luxembourg 🌐senat.fr/visite

Now the home of the French Senate, this palace was designed by Salomon de Brosse in the style of Florence's Pitti Palace to remind Marie de Médici, widow of Henri IV, of her native town. By the time it was finished (1631), Marie had been banished, but it remained a royal palace until the Revolution. In World War II, it was the headquarters of the Luftwaffe. The building is currently accessible to individual visitors only during the Heritage Days, which take place on the third weekend in September.

Jardin du Luxembourg

📍H9 🏠Blvd St-Michel/Rue de Vaugirard/Rue Guynemer 75006 Ⓜ Odéon 🚇Luxembourg ⏰Dawn–dusk daily 🌐senat.fr/visite/jardin

A green oasis covering 25 ha (60 acres) in the heart of the Left Bank, the Jardin du Luxembourg is one of the most popular parks in Paris. The landscaped

gardens are centred around the Palais du Luxembourg and feature an octagonal basin that is often surrounded by children sailing their wooden toy boats, which can be hired here. The Jardin du Luxembourg was created at the request of Marie de Médici, who had it designed as a fitting reminder of the Boboli Gardens at the Pitti Palace, in her home town of Florence. The original garden measured 8 ha (20 acres); what remains of it today are the large pond, the Fontaine Médicis and 2,000 elm trees. Statues were placed throughout the park in 1848. They include those of the queens of France, famous French women – Sainte Geneviève is an impressive example – and, later, famous writers and artists, too, adding up to 106 statues.

The garden is a great space for children, with activities such as a puppet theatre starring the famous character Guignol, a fenced-in playground, a carousel and tennis courts. Adults can play chess, wander through the engaging open-air photography

←

The stately Palais du Luxembourg in the gorgeous Jardin du Luxembourg

exhibitions or grab a chair and enjoy a free concert.

Fondation Cartier
📍H11 🏠261 Blvd Raspail 75014 Ⓜ️Raspail ⏰11am-8pm Tue-Sun (to 10pm Tue) 🚫1 Jan, 25 Dec 🌐fondationcartier.com
This foundation for contemporary art and architecture is housed in a building designed by Jean Nouvel. He has created an air of transparency and light, as well as incorporating a cedar of Lebanon, planted in 1823 by François-René de Chateaubriand. The structure complements the nature of the exhibitions of progressive art, which showcase personal, group or thematic displays.

Musée Zadkine
📍H10 🏠100 bis Rue d'Assas 75116 Ⓜ️Notre-Dame-des-Champs ⏰10am-6pm Tue-Sun 🚫Public hols 🌐zadkine.paris.fr
The Russian-born sculptor Ossip Zadkine lived here from 1928 until his death in 1967. The house, studio and garden contain his works. Here he produced his great commemorative sculpture *Ville Détruite*, commissioned by Rotterdam after World War II, and two monuments to Vincent van Gogh. The museum's works span the

development of Zadkine's style, from his Cubist beginnings to Expressionism and Abstractionism.

EAT

La Coupole
An Art Nouveau brasserie serving up meaty classics.

📍G10 🏠102 Blvd du Montparnasse 75014 🌐lacoupole-paris.com

€€€

Closerie des Lilas
A classic brasserie, once frequented by Hemingway.

📍H10 🏠171 Blvd du Montparnasse 75006 🌐closerie deslilas.fr

€€€

DRINK

Les Papilles
Wine bottles line the walls of this friendly local.

📍J9 🏠30 Rue Gay-Lussac 75005 🚫Sun, Mon 🌐lespapilles paris.fr

BEFORE YOU GO

Things change, so plan ahead to make the most of your trip. Be prepared for all eventualities by considering the following points before you travel.

AT A GLANCE

CURRENCY
Euro (EUR)

AVERAGE DAILY SPEND

SAVE	SPEND	SPLURGE
€65	€175	€300+

Bottled Water	Coffee	Beer	Dinner for Two
€1.50	€3.50	€8	€80

ESSENTIAL PHRASES

Hello	Bonjour
Goodbye	Au revoir
Please	S'il vous plaît
Thank you	Merci
Do you speak English	Parlez-vous anglais?
I don't understand	Je ne comprends pas

ELECTRICITY SUPPLY

Power sockets are type C and E, fitting two-pronged plugs. Standard voltage is 230 volts.

Passports and Visas

For entry requirements, consult your nearest French embassy or check the **France-Visas** website. Citizens of the UK, US, New Zealand, Canada and Australia do not need a visa for stays of up to three months but must apply in advance for the European Travel Information and Authorization System (**ETIAS**). Visitors from other countries may also require an ETIAS; check before travelling. EU nationals do not need a visa or an ETIAS.
ETIAS
W etiasvisa.com
France-Visas
W france-visas.gouv.fr

Government Advice

Make sure to consult both your and the French government beforehand. The **UK Foreign Commonwealth & Development Office (FCDO)**, the **US State Department**, the **Australian Department of Foreign Affairs and Trade** and **Gouvernement France** offer information on local laws.
Australian Department of Foreign Affairs and Trade
W smartraveller.gov.au
Gouvernement France
W gouvernement.fr
UK Foreign Commonwealth & Development Office (FCDO)
W gov.uk/foreign-travel-advice
US State Department
W travel.state.gov

Customs Information

Information on laws relating to goods and currency taken in or out of France is on the official **France customs** website.
France customs
W douane.gouv.fr

Insurance

We recommend that you take out a comprehensive insurance policy covering theft, loss of belongings, medical problems, cancellation and delays, and read the small print carefully.

EU and UK citizens are eligible for free emergency medical care in France, provided they have a valid EHIC (European Health Insurance Card) or **GHIC** (UK Global Health Insurance Card).

GHIC
W ghic.org.uk

Vaccinations

No inoculations are needed for France.

Booking Accommodation

Paris offers a variety of accommodation, including luxury five-star hotels, family-run B&Bs, budget hostels and private apartments. Tourists pour in from May to September, but Parisians pour out en masse in August.

Money

Most establishments accept major credit, debit and prepaid currency cards, but it's always a good idea to carry some cash too. Contactless payments are widely accepted.

Tipping generally isn't required, but it is considered polite to leave a few coins in recognition of good service.

Travellers with Specific Needs

Paris's historic buildings and cobbled streets can make the city tricky to navigate. However, there are many organizations working to improve accessibility in France's capital. The **Office du Tourisme et** lists accessible sights and routes for visitors with mobility issues, while **Jaccede** lists accessible museums, hotels, bars, restaurants and cinemas in Paris and other French cities.

Ile de France transport provides detailed information on accessible public transport, as well as a route planner, and **SNCF**'s website has information on accessible train travel.

Les Compagnons du Voyage will provide an escort for persons with limited mobility or visibility on public transport, for a fee.

Ile de France transport
W me-deplacer.iledefrance-mobilites.fr
Jaccede
W jaccede.com
Les Compagnons du Voyage
W compagnons.com
Office du Tourisme et
W parisjetaime.com
SNCF
W sncf-voyageurs.com

Language

French is the official language spoken in Paris. The French are fiercely proud of their language, but don't let this put you off. Mastering a few niceties goes a long way though you can get by without knowing the language at all.

Opening Hours

Situations can change quickly and unexpectedly. Always check before visiting attractions and hospitality venues for up-to-date opening hours and booking requirements.

Lunchtime Some local shops and businesses close for an hour or two from around noon.
Mondays Some museums, small shops, restaurants and bars are closed for the day.
Tuesdays National museums are closed for the day, except Versailles and the Musée d'Orsay, which are closed on Monday.
Sundays Most shops are closed.
Public holidays Public services, shops, museums and other attractions are usually closed.

GETTING AROUND

Paris has an efficient public transport system that will allow you to navigate the city's many sights with ease.

AT A GLANCE

PUBLIC TRANSPORT COSTS
Tickets are valid on all forms of public transport.

SINGLE

€2.10

(zones 1–3)

DAY TICKET

€8.45

(zones 1–3)

3-DAY TICKET

€33.10

(zones 1–3)

SPEED LIMIT

MOTORWAY

130 km/h
(80 mph)

MAJOR ROADS

80 km/h
(49 mph)

RING ROADS

70 km/h
(43 mph)

URBAN AREAS

50 km/h
(30 mph)

Arriving by Air

Paris has two major airports, Charles de Gaulle (also known as Roissy) and Orly, and one secondary airport, Beauvais, which serves mainly budget airlines. All three are well connected to the city centre by train, bus and taxi. Car hire facilities are also available, although driving in Paris is not recommended. For information on journey times and ticket prices between airports and the city centre, see the table opposite.

Airport Shuttle is a site that searches for the best offers for services, including shared rides and private drivers, between the airports and your destination. It provides up-to-date prices for buses, taxis and all other options, allowing travellers to find what fits their budget.

The **RATP Roissybus** operates regular services from Charles de Gaulle, and RER trains (Line B) leave regularly every 5–15 minutes, calling at Gare du Nord, Châtelet-Les-Halles and other major stations. In June 2024 an extension to Metro Line 14 was inaugurated, connecting Orly with central Paris. The journey time to Gare de Lyon will be around 25 minutes. The most direct way into Paris from Beauvais is by shuttle bus to Porte-Maillot. It is wise to book the 90-minute journey in advance online.

Airport Shuttle
🅦 airportshuttles.com
RATP Roissybus
🅦 parisaeroport.fr

Train Travel

International Train Travel
Regular high-speed trains connect Paris's six international railway stations to major cities across Europe. Reservations for these services are essential, as seats get booked up quickly, particularly during peak times.

You can buy tickets and passes for multiple international journeys from **Eurail** or **Interrail**; however, you may need to pay an additional reservation fee. Always check carefully before boarding that your pass is valid on the service you wish to use.

Eurostar runs a fast service from London to central Paris via the Channel Tunnel.

Students and those under 26 can benefit from discounted rail travel both to and within France. For more information, visit the Eurail or Interrail website.

Thalys runs a high-speed service between Paris, Brussels and Amsterdam ten times a day, with a variety of special offers, package deals and half-price last-minute deals.

Eurail
W eurail.com
Eurostar
W eurostar.com
Interrail
W interrail.eu
Thalys
W thalys.com

Domestic Train Travel

Paris has a number of main train stations situated at various points across the city, all of which serve different regions.

The French state railway, **SNCF**, has two services in Paris: the Banlieue suburban service and the Grandes Lignes, or long-distance service. The suburban services all operate within the five-zone network. The long-distance services operate throughout France. The TGV offers a high-speed service that should be booked in advance. There are also a number of budget high-speed trains, such as **Ouigo**.

Before boarding a train, time-punch (composter) tickets to validate your journey; this does not apply for e-tickets. Tickets for city transport cannot be used on Banlieue trains, with the exception of some RER tickets to stations with both SNCF and RER lines.

Ouigo
W ouigo.com
SNCF
W oui.sncf.com

Public Transport

The Metro, RER, buses and trams are all run by **RATP** (Régie Autonome des Transports Parisiens). Safety and hygiene measures, timetables, ticket information, transport maps and more can be found on their website.

RATP
W ratp.fr

Tickets

The Paris metropolitan area is divided into five ticket zones. Central Paris is zone 1, Charles de Gaulle airport is in zone 5, Orly airport and Versailles in zone 4. The Metro serves zones 1–3.

To avoid buying paper tickets (which are being phased out by 2025) you can either buy tickets on your phone using the RATP app (Bonjour RATP) or get a **Navigo** pass, a rechargeable smart card that can be used on the Metro, RER and buses. The Navigo Easy costs €2 for the pass and can be topped up with credit and with as many standard fares as you like.

Visitors can enjoy unlimited travel on the Metro, RER and Paris buses with a Paris Visite pass, valid for one, two, three or five consecutive days in zones 1–3, or a one-day Mobilis card, valid in the zones of your choice for one day. Children under four travel free, while children aged four to nine travel half price. Bus-only tickets can be purchased on board from the driver. All bus tickets must be validated using the machine on the bus.

Navigo
W ratp.fr

Metro and RER

The Paris Metro has 14 main lines and two minor lines. The RER is a system of five lines of commuter trains that travel underground in central Paris and above ground in outlying areas. The two systems overlap in the city centre. RER trips outside the centre require special tickets; fares to suburbs and nearby towns vary.

Buses and Trams

Most buses must be flagged down at designated stops. Your ticket may be used for transfers to other bus and tramway lines for 90 minutes (between the first and last validation). Each time you change buses or trams, you must validate your ticket again. Exceptions to this rule are the Orlybus and Roissybus services, and lines 221, 297, 299, 350 and 351.

There are 47 night bus lines, called Noctilien, serving Paris and its suburbs. The terminus for most lines is Châtelet. Thirteen tram lines, T1 to T13, operate in Paris, mainly servicing the outskirts of the city. You can travel on the trams using regular Metro tickets and passes. They don't run past most major tourist attractions but can be a pleasant way to see the outer reaches of Paris.

Long-Distance Bus Travel

Two major coach operators, **Flixbus** and **BlaBlaBus**, link Paris to other towns in France and destinations throughout Europe. They are low-cost alternatives to planes and trains – travellers from Paris may reach London, Brussels, Amsterdam, Milan and Barcelona, as well as Warsaw, Zagreb and Bucharest, among other cities.

BlaBlaBus
🖥 blablacar.fr/bus
Flixbus
🖥 flixbus.co.uk

Taxis

Taxis can be hailed in the street or from one of the 500 or so taxi ranks dotted around the city. Fares start at around €6.60 for an immediate booking and around €9.60 for prior booking. There is usually an additional charge for more than three passengers.

Vélo taxis are convenient, motorized tricycle rickshaws that offer a green alternative to traditional taxis. **G7 Taxis** has a large fleet of electric and hybrid cars. If you're after a motorcycle taxi, book with **CityBird**. Taxi apps such as Uber, Free Now and Bolt also operate in Paris.

Citybird
🖥 city-bird.com
G7 Taxis
🖥 g7.fr

Driving

Driving in Paris is not recommended. Traffic is often heavy, there are many one-way streets and parking is notoriously difficult, not to mention expensive.

Driving to Paris

Autoroutes (motorways) converge on Paris from all directions. For those travelling from Britain to Paris by road, the simplest way is to use the Eurotunnel trains that run between the terminals at Folkestone and Calais, which both have direct motorway access. Paris is surrounded by an outer ring road called the Boulevard Périphérique. All motorways leading to the capital link in to the Périphérique. Each former city gate (*porte*) now corresponds to an exit onto or from the Périphérique. Arriving motorists should take time to check their destination address and consult a map of central Paris to find the closest corresponding *porte*.

Car Rental

To hire a car in France you must be 21 or over and have held a valid driver's licence for at least a year. You will also need to present a credit card to secure the hire deposit. Check the laws regarding the type licence you need to drive in France with your local automobile association beforehand.

Ada.Paris is a self-service car hire service that operates in the Paris region. You can pick up a car from a parking station, make your journey and park at any other station.
Ada.Paris
🖥 ada.fr

Driving in Paris

Paris is a limited traffic zone and it is compulsory for all vehicles to display a Crit'Air sticker with a number ranging from

1 to 5, which denotes the level of pollution. In the event of high pollution levels, vehicles with certain stickers may be banned from the road. Stickers can be purchased from the **Air Quality Certificate Service**. Park in areas with a large "P" or *payant* sign on the pavement or road, and pay at the parking meter with *La Paris Carte* (available from any kiosk), a credit or debit card, or using the PaybyPhone app.

Paris has numerous underground car parks, signposted by a white "P" on a blue background.

Air Quality Certificate Service
W certificat-air.gouv.fr

Rules of the Road

Always drive on the right. Unless otherwise signposted, vehicles coming from the right have right of way. Cars on a roundabout usually have right of way, although the Arc de Triomphe is a hair-raising exception as cars give way to traffic on the right.

Drivers must carry a valid driver's licence, registration and insurance documents. Wearing of seat belts is compulsory, and it is prohibited to sound your horn in the city. For motorbikes and scooters, the wearing of helmets and protective gloves is compulsory. In the city centre, it is against the law to use the bus lanes at any time of day. France strictly enforces its drink-drive limit.

Boats and Ferries

Arriving by Sea
The following companies run passenger and vehicle ferry services from the UK: **P&O Ferries** runs services from Dover to Calais, **Condor Ferries** operates between Poole and St-Malo and **DFDS Seaways** runs routes from Newhaven to Dieppe and from Dover to Dunkirk. **Brittany Ferries** makes crossings from Plymouth to Roscoff, from Poole and Portsmouth to Cherbourg, and from Portsmouth to Le Havre and Caen. They also run an overnight service from Portsmouth to St-Malo.

Driving to Paris from Cherbourg takes four hours; from Dieppe or Le Havre, two and a half hours; and from Calais, two hours.

Brittany Ferries
W brittany-ferries.co.uk

Condor Ferries
W condorferries.co.uk

DFDS Seaways
W dfds.com

P&O Ferries
W poferries.com

Paris by Boat
Paris's river-boat shuttle, the **Batobus**, runs every 20–45 minutes, with more frequent services in spring and summer. Tickets can be bought at Batobus stops, RATP and tourist offices.

Batobus
W batobus.com

Cycling

Paris is reasonably flat, manageably small and has many backstreets where traffic is restricted. The city now has around 1,000 km (620 miles) of cycle lanes, making exploring by bike easier and safer than ever. This is set to increase hugely over the next few years, with the aim of making the city "100 per cent cyclable" by 2026.

Bicycle Hire
The **Vélib'** shared bicycle scheme is available 24 hours a day. There are over 1,400 Vélib' docking terminals dotted throughout the Greater Paris area; payment is made via the smartphone app or by credit card at the terminals. The first 45 minutes are €3, increasing by €1 for every additional half hour. Electric bikes cost only a little extra.

Vélib'
W velib-metropole.fr

Bicycle Tours
Bike About Tours offer trips to Paris's most famous landmarks and to offbeat locations.

Bike About Tours
W bikeabouttours.com

PRACTICAL INFORMATION

A little local know-how goes a long way in Paris. Here you will find all the essential advice and information you will need during your stay.

EMERGENCY NUMBERS

GENERAL EMERGENCY	FIRE SERVICE AND AMBULANCE
112	**18**

POLICE	MEDICAL EMERGENCY
17	**15**

TIME ZONE
CET/CEST
Central European
Summer Time
(CEST) runs from
end Mar to end Oct.

TAP WATER
Unless stated
otherwise, tap
water in France
is safe to drink.

WEBSITES

parisjetaime.com
The official Paris tourist board website.

Le Fooding
Use this app to find the nearest
recommended restaurant in an instant.

PaybyPhone
Pay for on-street parking easily.

Bonjour RATP
Official app of RATP, the city's public
transport operator.

Personal Security

Paris is generally a safe city to visit. Petty theft is as common here as in most major cities. Pickpockets often frequent tourist spots and wander the Metro system and RER so guard your belongings at all times. To report a theft, go to the nearest police station (commissariat de police) within 24 hours, and bring ID with you. A list of police stations can be found on the Office du Tourisme website. Get a copy of the crime report in order to claim on your insurance. If you have your passport stolen, or in the event of a serious crime or accident, contact your embassy.

As a rule, Parisians are accepting of all people, regardless of their race, gender or sexuality. Same-sex marriage was legalized in 2013 and France recognized the right to legally change your gender in 2016. Paris has a thriving LGBTQ+ scene, centred in the Marais district. The **Centre LGBT Paris Ile-de-France** offers advice and hosts regular events. Events in recent years have led to an increased army and police presence in Paris, which should be regarded as normal. Expect bag checks at most major attractions.
Centre LGBT Paris Ile-de-France
🅦 centrelgbtparis.org

Health

Emergency healthcare is free for all EU nationals with an EHIC card. You may have to pay for treatment and reclaim the money later. For visitors from outside the EU, payment of medical expenses is the patient's responsibility; make sure to arrange comprehensive medical insurance beforehand. Paris hospitals are listed on the **Assistance Publique** website. Hôtel Dieu (Pl du Parvis Notre-Dame) is the most centrally located hospital. In case of a dental emergency,

SOS Dentaire will provide a prompt house
call, but be prepared to pay a substantial fee.
The **Centre Médical Europe** also has a dental
practice. A green cross indicates a pharmacy.
As well as selling medicines, pharmacies
advise on minor health problems and can
give details of the nearest doctor. You can
usually find details of the nearest 24-hour
service on all pharmacy doors.

Assistance Publique
W aphp.fr
Centre Médical Europe
W centre-medical-europe.fr
SOS Dentaire
W sosdentaire.com

Smoking, Alcohol and Drugs

Smoking is prohibited in public places, but
is allowed on café and pub terraces, as long
as they are not enclosed. The possession
of narcotics is prohibited and could result in
a prison sentence. Unless stated otherwise,
alcohol consumption on the streets is per-
mitted. France has a strict limit of 0.05 per
cent BAC (blood alcohol content) for drivers.

ID

There is no requirement for visitors to carry
ID, but in the event of a routine check you
may be asked to show your passport. If you
don't have it with you, the police may escort
you to where your passport is kept.

Local Customs

Etiquette (*la politesse*) is important to
Parisians. On entering a store or café, you
are expected to say *"bonjour"* to staff, and
au revoir" when leaving. Be sure to add *"s'il
vous plaît"* (please) when ordering something
and *"pardon"* if you bump into someone.
 The French usually shake hands on
meeting someone for the first time. Friends
and colleagues who know each other well
greet each other with a kiss on each cheek. If
you are unsure what's expected, wait to
see if they proffer a hand or a cheek.

Visiting Churches and Cathedrals

Dress respectfully. Cover your torso and
upper arms; ensure shorts and skirts cover
your knees.

Mobile Phones and Wi-Fi

Free Wi-Fi hotspots provide fast internet
access in over 260 public places in Paris,
including museums, parks and libraries.
Cafés and restaurants usually permit the
use of their Wi-Fi if you make a purchase.
 Visitors travelling to Paris with EU tariffs
will be able to use their devices without
data roaming charges.

Post

Stamps can be bought at post offices and
tabacs. Most post offices have self-service
machines to weigh and frank your mail.

Taxes and Refunds

VAT is around 20% in France. Non-EU
residents can claim back tax on certain goods.
Look out for the Global Refund Tax-Free
sign, where the retailer will supply a form
and issue a *détaxe* receipt. Present the goods
and *détaxe* receipt and passport at customs
when you depart to receive your refund.

Discount Cards

Entry to some national and municipal
museums is free on the first Sunday of each
month. Visitors under 18 years of age and
EU passport holders aged 18–26 years are
usually admitted free, and there are sometimes discounts for students and over-60s
who have ID showing their date of birth. The
Paris Pass offers access to over 60 attractions for two, four or six days and offers
unlimited travel on the Metro, buses and
RER within central Paris, and a ticket for a
hop-on hop-off bus tour.
Paris Pass
W parispass.com

INDEX

ACKNOWLEDGMENTS

DK would like to thank the following for their contribution to the previous edition: Dipika Dasgupta, Shikha Kulkarni, Aryan Pirolli, Hollie Teague, Priyanka Thakur, Alan Tillier.

The publisher would like to thank the following for their kind permission to reproduce their photographs:

key: a-above; b-below/bottom; c-centre; f-far; l-left; r-right; t-top

Alamy Stock Photo: Piere Monbon 94b; hemis.fr / Guiziou Franck 20b, / Bertrand Gardel 54b, 41tl, / Gilles Rigoulet 97tl, Sonnet Sylvain 13tl, 18tl; Brian Jannsen 70–71t; Boris Karpinski 59clb; John Kellerman 55tl, 31br, 84clb; Iugris 21tr; Samantha Ohlsen 92bl; Photo 12 / Gilles Targat 57br; Frederic Reglain 19b; robertharding / JP Merten 21clb; RossHelen Editorial 75r; Street Art 34b.

AWL Images: Jon Arnold 28b, / Tour Eiffel- Illuminations Pierre Bideau 64b. Cité Des Sciences et de L'industrie: EPPDCSI / E Luider 42t. © DACS 2019: © ADAGP, Paris and DACS, London 2018 40b, 44br; © DB-ADAGP Paris and DACS, London 2018 61t; © Succession Picasso / DACS, London 2018 13tl. Dreamstime.com: Andersastphoto 63br; Andrey Andronov 62tl; Antoine2k 29t; Astormfr 6b; Bargotiphotography 73tl; Nicolas De Corte 48bl; Ionut David 98b; Matthew Dixon 68bl; Dennis Dolkens 32–3t; Tatiana Dyuvbanova 47br; Evolove 74b; Ioana Grecu 76tr; Infomods 78–9bc; Valerijs Jegorovs 54br; Aliaksandr Kazlou 35br; Kmiragaya 100br; Sergii Kolesnyk 53t; Denys Kuvaiev 39br; Madrabothair 10tl, 36br, 56t; Tomas Marek 99t; Minacarson 27bc, 61t; Luciano Mortula 88b; MrFly 65t; Neirfy 2t; Nui7711 17tr;

Kovalenkov Petr 25b; Elena Ska 4–5b; Spytsekouras 91tl; Darius Strazdas 22bl, 35tl; Tigger76 12b; Worakan Thaomor 67bl; Uatp1 59cr; Ukrphoto 81crb; UlyssePixel 26–7b; VanderWolf-Images 52b; Dennis Van De Water 95t. Getty Images: Moment / Photo by Ivan Vukelic 58b; Photolibrary / Julian Elliott Photography 80b. Getty Images / iStock: Alpamayo-Photo 46b; E+ / Orbon Alija 3tl, / Pavliha 72b; johnkellerman 86t; JoselgnacioSoto 7cra; Valerie Loiseleux 50tr; MarioGuti 82b; Sean3810 7clb. Musée de Louvre: © Pyramide du Louvre, arch. I. M. Pei 58b. Le Musée du Quai Branly - Jacques Chirac: Lois Lammerhuber 66t. SuperStock: hemis.fr / Gardel Bertrand 40b, 44br.

Illustrations and all other images © Dorling Kindersley Limited
For further information see: www.dkimages.com

PHRASE BOOK

IN AN EMERGENCY

Help!	Au secours!	oh sekoor
Stop!	Arrêtez!	aret-ay
Call a doctor!	Appelez un médecin!	apuh-lay uñ medsañ
Call an ambulance!	Appelez une ambulance!	apuh-lay oon oñboñ-loñs
Call the police!	Appelez la police!	apuh-lay lah poh-lees
Call the fire brigade!	Appelez les pompiers!	apuh-lay leh poñ-peeyay
Where is the nearest telephone?	Où est le téléphone le plus proche?	oo ay luh tehlehfon luh ploo prosh
Where is the nearest hospital?	Où est l'hôpital le plus proche?	oo ay lopeetal luh ploo prosh

COMMUNICATION ESSENTIALS

Yes	Oui	wee
No	Non	noñ
Please	S'il vous plaît	seel voo play
Thank you	Merci	mer-see
Excuse me	Excusez-moi	exkoo-zay mwah
Hello	Bonjour	boñzhoor
Goodbye	Au revoir	oh ruh-vwar
Good night	Bonsoir	boñ-swar
Morning	Le matin	matañ
Afternoon	L'après-midi	l'apreh-meedee
Evening	Le soir	swar
Yesterday	Hier	eeyehr
Today	Aujourd'hui	oh-zhoor-dwee
Tomorrow	Demain	duhmañ
Here	Ici	ee-see
There	Là	lah
What?	Quoi, quel, quelle?	kwah, kel, kel
When?	Quand?	koñ
Why?	Pourquoi?	poor-kwah
Where?	Où?	oo

USEFUL PHRASES

How are you?	Comment allez-vous?	kom-moñ talay voo
Very well, thank you.	Très bien, merci.	treh byañ, mer-see
Pleased to meet you.	Enchanté de faire votre connaissance.	oñshoñ-tay duh fehr votr kon-ay-sans
See you soon.	A bientôt.	byañ-toh
That's fine	C'est bon	say bon
Where is/are...?	Où est/sont...?	ooay/soñ
How far is it to...?	Combien de kilometres d'ici à...?	kom-byañ duh keelo-metr d'ee-see ah
Which way to...?	Quelle est la direction pour...?	kel ay lah deer-ek-syoñ poor
Do you speak English?	Parlez-vous anglais?	par-lay voo oñg-lay
I don't understand.	Je ne comprends pas.	zhuh nuh kom-proñ pah
Could you speak slowly please?	Pouvez-vous parler moins vite s'il vous plaît?	poo-vay voo par-lay mwañ veet seel voo play
I'm sorry.	Excusez-moi.	exkoo-zay mwah

USEFUL WORDS

big	grand	groñ
small	petit	puh-tee
hot	chaud	show
cold	froid	frwah
good	bon/bien	boñ/byañ
bad	mauvais	moh-veh
enough	assez	assay
well	bien	byañ
open	ouvert	oo-ver
closed	fermé	fer-meh
left	gauche	gohsh
right	droite	drwaht
early	de bonne heure	duh bon urr
late	en retard	oñ ruh-tar
entrance	l'entrée	l'on-tray
exit	la sortie	sor-tee
toilet	les toilettes, le WC	twah-let, vay-see
Unoccupied free, no charge	libre gratuit	leebr grah-twee

Manifestation
Tarot

Make your dreams become your reality with the power and insight of the Tarot

XX Judgment
I know my destiny

VI The Lovers
I am supported by love

XIX The Sun
I am full of hope

Jayne Wallace

Illustrations by Julia C...

CICO BOOK
LONDON NEW YO...

Acknowledgments

I would like to thank CICO Books for all their work. Many thanks to Chelsea, my book agent, and all my team at Psychic Sisters, Selfridges, for their ongoing support.

Published in 2024 by CICO Books
An imprint of Ryland Peters & Small Ltd
20–21 Jockey's Fields   341 E 116th St
London WC1R 4BW   New York, NY 10029

www.rylandpeters.com

10 9 8 7 6 5 4 3 2 1

Text © Jayne Wallace 2024
Illustrations © Julia Cellini 2024
Design © CICO Books 2024
Citrine crystal photograph (page 6) by Roy Palmer
and Geoff Dann, © CICO Books 2024

A CIP catalog record for this book is available from the Library of Congress and the British Library.

ISBN: 978 1 80065 373 3

Printed in China

In-house editor: Jenny Dye
Senior designer: Emily Breen
Art director: Sally Powell
Creative director: Leslie Harrington
Production manager: Gordana Simakovic
Publishing manager: Carmel Edmonds

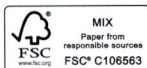

XVIII The Moon
I find the way in the darkness

XII The Hanged Man
I am enlightened

MIX
Paper from responsible sources
FSC® C106563

Contents

Introduction

Have you ever noticed how certain people seem to have the golden touch? For the super-successful, it can seem like riches and opportunities just magically fall into their laps. Chances are, these seemingly lucky folk are using the art of manifestation—be it consciously or subconsciously—to attract good things.

Manifestation harnesses the Law of Attraction to enable us to live happy, prosperous lives. This universal law has its roots in ancient philosophies such as Buddhism. It states that like attracts like. And that includes energy. Every particle of our being vibrates with energy. Positivity—a good attitude and happy thoughts—makes our bodies and spirits vibrate at a higher frequency, and we manifest wonderful abundance. A negative mindset can bring the opposite. The good news is the Law of Attraction is something you can control!

Want a real-life example of how this works? When I was a kid, my family didn't have much money. I struggled with schoolwork and was labeled stupid—in fact, I have dyslexia. Juvenile rheumatoid arthritis left me in near-constant pain. The expectation from others was that I wouldn't amount to much. That wasn't my belief though. I always knew that I would be successful. In fact, in my head, it had already happened. I didn't know it at the time, but I was manifesting!

Fast-forward to the present-day. It has happened! With my Psychic Sisters franchise in Selfridges, one of London's most prestigious stores, TV appearances, and a new business launch, my life is prospering in a fantastic way. I travel to the US, appear on TV shows, read for A-list celebrities, and my Psychic Sisters reiki-energized wellness products are on the shelves countrywide in the UK. Using the art of manifestation, I create my reality every day—and you can, too.

The brilliant thing about manifesting is, even if you're a worrier or a negative Nelly, using this deck you can switch your mindset from scarcity to abundance and super-charge your manifestation potential. Not only will each card give you psychic insight, it will also give you the tools to raise your energy vibration and make your dreams become your best reality.

You are in control of your destiny. Once you've aligned yourself with the Law of Attraction, there will be no need to struggle for what you're aiming for. Just trust in the process and things will happen smoothly. Manifesting means people come into your life at the right time, and opportunities will appear. Are you ready to raise your vibration and make the magic happen? Let's begin!

Preparing Your Cards

After opening your cards, rub your hands with an essential oil. My favorite is lavender oil, which unblocks any negative emotions that might stand in the way of intentions. Shuffle the cards, then wrap them up in a silk scarf—choose a vibrant shade of gold or green, the colors of abundance, wealth attraction, and growth. Connect to your cards by sleeping with them under your pillow for three nights. The number three has particular significance, as it is a direct link to the Universe and a symbol of the divine. Light a candle and repeat, "I am connected to my cards," three times. You are ready to begin reading the cards.

The Flower of Manifestation

On the back of the cards you will see the flower of manifestation, unfurling to reveal the beautiful possibilities the Universe is offering. It is the lotus, sacred in many Eastern cultures and a symbol of purity, spiritual enlightenment, and rebirth. In Hinduism, it represents the womb of the Universe from which all things are born. Seven petals radiate out. Each petal represents a major chakra. "Chakra" means "wheel" in Sanskrit and refers to the body's energy centers. The seven chakra colors on the petals each represent a part of the body, going from the root to the crown. Ultimately, this flower represents faith in ourselves.

Seven-day Challenge

You can use your deck to do any Tarot spread (see pages 6–10), but a great way to kickstart your connection to the Rule of Attraction is to try a Manifestation Challenge. In the morning, using only the Major Arcana (0 to XXI), shuffle the cards and pick one, then use the card's mantra as an affirmation for the day. For example, if you pick The Empress, the mantra is "I am abundant." Say it out loud seven times quickly to give your intention energy. Take note of how you recognize abundance coming into your life over the next 24 hours. Perhaps you get an unexpected gift, or someone does you a favor. Write down your observations. Repeat the process for seven days. At the end of the week, look at the story your cards have told you. The Universe has given you a blueprint of where you should be heading in life at the moment.

Manifesting Tip: Say It Out Loud

One of my manifesting secrets is to say things out loud. By doing this, you are putting your intention out to the Universe. Here is an amazing example of what I mean. In 2005, I sat in the coffee shop in Selfridges in London, shuffling my Tarot cards, chatting to a friend about my work. "I'm going to have a shop here," I told her. At this point I was doing well and appearing in magazines, but a spot in the store feted as the best in the world? Could that really happen? Even I was amazed by the speed of what happened next. The boss of Selfridges spotted me with my Tarot cards and was curious. He came over and started chatting. Boom! Two weeks later I got a shot doing readings in-store and continue to do so.

Reading the Cards

When you are ready to lay out a reading, find a quiet, uncluttered space. Choose which spread you would like to try (see pages 6–10). Try burning incense such as sage to spiritually purify the room. Light a candle and turn on music that soothes you and helps you to connect to your intuition—this helps you to "see" or be aware of what you want to manifest. Try holding the crystal citrine, the stone of manifestation, or a diamond, which is known to amplify energies, before a reading. Shuffle the cards and consider what you want from this reading. Be clear and ask the Universe out loud for it. For example, "I want to know the steps I need to take to lead me to my soulmate," or, "Give me guidance that this job offer is a good fit for me." After you have completed the reading, thank the Universe for the guidance.

Embracing manifestation requires aligning with the Universe's energy. So, repeat a mantra three times, depending on what you are trying to discover. It could be, "The world is blessing me with love," "I am open to new, creative possibilities," or, "I make room for financial abundance"—you're signaling to the psychic energies around you what you are manifesting.

Spread the cards face down in a fan shape, selecting those you feel most drawn to until you have the number needed for your chosen spread. Alternatively, cut the deck into three face-down piles, and choose the one you feel most guided to. Gather the other two piles together and place your chosen pile on top; then, when selecting the cards, draw from the top. Place the rest of the deck to one side, and turn the chosen cards over one at a time.

One-card Reading

Start with the simplicity of the one-card reading, allowing it to be a beacon for immediate guidance or a daily affirmation. This practice is not merely about seeking answers but also about setting intentions and inviting the Universe to manifest your desires and insights for the day.

After preparing for the reading, shuffle your cards with purpose, inviting insight to flow. If a specific question stirs, gently repeat it in your mind as you shuffle. Draw your card with intention and check its meaning in this book. Write down the card's message, along with any intuitive thoughts, in a manifestation journal. If you're not sure what the message means, return to it after a week or longer, depending on the timescale of the situation. When you look back, you will often spot the message.

Past, Present, Future

This three-card spread is a powerful way to connect the dots when it comes to where your life is heading. Use this layout to delve into a specific matter or to invite a broader

CITRINE CRYSTAL

understanding of the currents moving through your life. You can also use this spread for a more general reading about themes you should look out for, and for focusing on how to allow your cherished dream to become a reality.

The first card reflects the past, shedding light on events that have shaped your current circumstances or continue to affect you. The second card captures the present, highlighting the challenges and influences of today, guiding you on the path forward. The third card offers a glimpse into the future, suggesting an outcome from your current course. Check the meanings of the cards using this guidebook. Whatever the result, remember that the future isn't fixed;

1. PAST   2. PRESENT   3. FUTURE

it evolves with your decisions and mindset—you have the power to manifest the future you want.

Staircase of Success

Achieving a goal is often a series of steps. Perhaps you are manifesting a brilliant new career or a lasting relationship, but you're looking for signposts on how it's going to happen. This is where the Staircase of Success comes into its own. It's a way of seeing how your future is going to unfold in a timeframe, usually a year, but it can be a shorter or a longer period—the choice is yours. A tip: make sure you use the floor or a large table or you might run out of space.

Place the first card to represent a period of time, say a month, horizontally. Then place another card next to it but an inch forward. And another. Soon you will see a staircase reaching upward. Now turn the cards over and see how and where the steps of success are going to take you!

1

2

3—And so on...

Manifest Pyramid

The geometry of the pyramid is well known to be able to transform energy. The shape allows weight to be distributed throughout the structure. Most of the weight in a pyramid is on the bottom and it decreases the higher up you go.

In fact, the triangular shape of the pyramid has symbolic and spiritual significance in many belief systems. Similar to the birth, life, and death cycle, the triangle signifies that everything in life has a start, a process, and an ending. This three-sided shape is commonly associated with the stages of growth, leading to an elevated state of existence. In a spiritual sense, it denotes a journey toward enlightenment or a bond with a universal entity. From an energetic perspective, triangles channel power in their pointed direction. If you wish to manifest more into your life, this sacred spread can boost your chances.

Place the cards as shown—your cards should form a perfect triangle, maximizing the powerful spiritual symmetry—then follow the interpretations below.

2. THE JOURNEY   3. MANIFESTATION

1. FOUNDATION

1. Foundation
This card indicates where you're coming from. This may be from a place of hardship, or perhaps you have loving supporters or advantages. The card you draw here will give a reflection of this.

2. The Journey
What do you need to do to achieve your dream? Whether it's old-fashioned hard work, enlisting the help of influential people, or looking out for serendipitous strokes of fortune, this card will give you a clue.

3. Manifestation
What will be the outcome of your current path? This card shows what can be made real. As ever, if the card is not what you were expecting, remember that you have the power to make your future. But sit with the message first and check whether the Universe is telling you something. In my opinion, even cards with imagery that unnerves us are not bad. Perhaps, if you draw the Tower for example, total transformation is actually something rather wonderful.

Tree of Life

The Tree of Life Tarot spread is a deeply symbolic layout drawn from the Kabbalistic Tree of Life, a symbol of the Universe's structure and the spiritual journey, making it perfect for manifestation. Each position in the Tree of Life enables you to go deeper and see your psychological motivations, to enable greater insight and understanding of the forces that shape life. It consists of ten cards, each representing different aspects of the person's life and spiritual path, including aspects of wisdom, understanding, compassion, strength, and so on.

Before you begin, ensure you are in a quiet, meditative space. Shuffle your Tarot deck while focusing on your question or intention. Place the cards as shown and follow the interpretations below.

Consider how the cards interact with each other and the overall flow of the spread when you are thinking about the interpretation. Muse on the message it is sending—and remember you are in charge of manifesting your destiny.

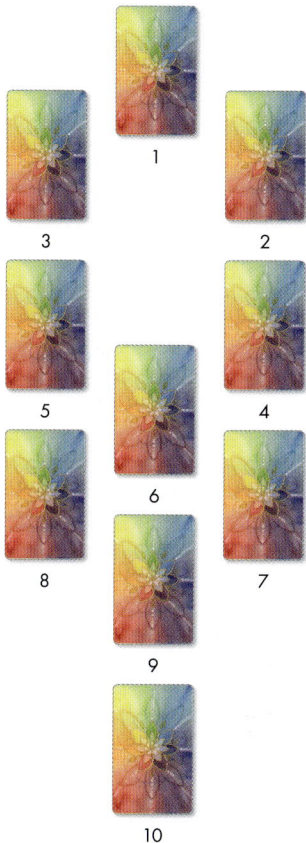

Card 1 represents the highest outcome—what you should be bringing into your life through manifestation.

Cards 2 and 3 represent the forces of wisdom and understanding that shape your life.

Card 4 relates to obstacles.

Cards 5 and 6 are your inner strength and compassion respectively.

Card 7 shows your world, what you have, and potential talents.

Card 8 represents how you show yourself to the world.

Card 9 is the heavens, giving you a signpost to how to manifest your heart's desire.

Card 10 represents the material world, the outcome of all the above energies in your everyday life.

The Pentagram

The Pentagram—the five-pointed star—may have been maligned as being connected with the dark arts, but this is a misunderstanding. It represents nature and the world, and where we sit in this wonderful Universe. It was used in ancient Mesopotamia and by the Hebrews as a symbol of truth. You can trace its inclusion in the amulets of various cultures.

In Pagan and Wiccan traditions, the Pentagram is a symbol of the elements—Earth, Air, Fire, Water, and Spirit. It's often used as a protective symbol and a representation of the interconnectedness of all things. In essence, the Pentagram represents wholeness, which makes it a brilliant blueprint for a Tarot reading. Using its magical properties can help you manifest your dreams. Place the cards as shown and follow the interpretations below.

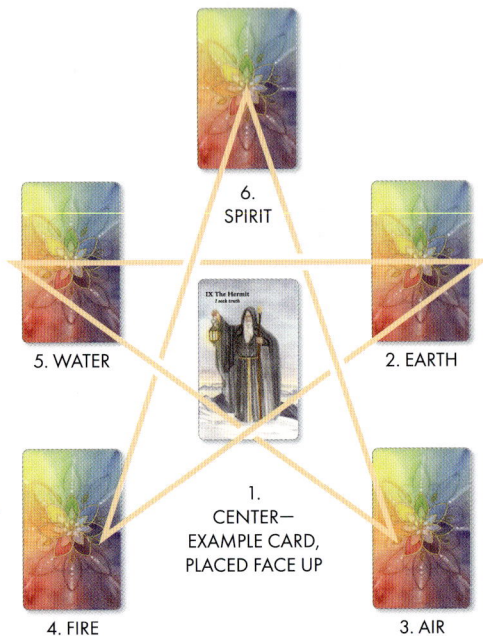

6. SPIRIT

5. WATER

2. EARTH

1. CENTER—EXAMPLE CARD, PLACED FACE UP

4. FIRE

3. AIR

1. Center—current state of mind
Actively choose a card from the Major Arcana—which card represents your current state of mind? Are you in flux at the moment? Perhaps you're feeling introverted, so the Hermit would be appropriate. If you're feeling like life is on pause, The Hanged Man could be the card. Place this card face up.

2. Earth
The element Earth is associated with security and stability. It represents the overall issues that are being faced. What is causing you to feel stuck? Look for clues about how you can transform this into positivity.

3. Air
Air is associated with communication, inspiration, and intuition. This position looks at how others are influencing the situation. Are they having a positive or negative effect? Understand the personalities at play so you can get to your goal.

4. Fire
Fire embodies strong will and energy. Fire can both create and destroy. Are there internal conflicts at play here? Discover ways to channel this fiery energy for the good.

5. Water
Water is associated with wisdom, emotions, and intuition. Tap into what your higher self is telling you. It shows what can be learned from the situation. How can you adapt to meet future goals?

6. Spirit
This is the whole self, the culmination of the journey, and what all the other cards are leading up to. Look at the previous four cards, representing the four elements, and see the story of how your best future will manifest itself.

The Major Arcana

A Tarot deck contains a pack of 78 illustrated cards, each depicting specific symbols and characters. The Tarot originated in Italy during the 15th century. The Major Arcana in Tarot is a set of 22 cards, each with its own symbolism, story, and archetype. These cards are considered the core and foundation of the deck, representing various aspects of the human experience and spiritual journey, starting with The Fool and completing the arc with The World.

Using the Major Arcana for manifestation involves meditating on each card's symbolism and incorporating its lessons into your daily life. Each card offers us a learning opportunity—play with the cards and you will learn so much.

You can use the cards as tools for reflection, decision-making, and guiding your path toward your desired outcomes. Each card embodies a powerful archetype or lesson that can help clarify your intentions, make informed decisions, and foster a deeper understanding of yourself and the world around you. By working with the Major Arcana, you align yourself with the energies and stories they represent, aiding in personal growth and the manifestation of your goals.

For example, The Magician, the ultimate manifestation card, can transform intent and energy into manifesting your desires. The Hierophant advises you to make dreams become a reality by seeking wisdom and guidance from trusted mentors. Even The Devil can enable us to embrace change and let go of the old to make way for the new.

Each card comes with its own rich symbolism and magical mantra for manifestation, including numerological meaning. If you're new to Tarot, try focusing first on the Major Arcana and enjoy exploring the power of the cards and how they can reveal your best future.

0 The Fool
I have faith

XXI The World
I am successful

0 The Fool

0 The Fool
I have faith

Keywords: *New beginnings, faith, travel, change, trust, protection*

Mantra:

I have faith.

A carefree young person stands at the edge of a cliff, about to step into the unknown. The Fool embodies the archetype of the hero's journey, embarking on an adventure, leaving behind the safety of their known world to explore uncharted territory. This journey is filled with challenges, lessons, and transformations. The Fool carries a small bag representing the experiences and lessons they will collect on their journey. The card's number 0 is symbolic of limitless potential in numerology—a blank canvas that can be filled with wonder. You can go from zero to hero! A small dog accompanies the Fool. This represents our animal sense of intuition and inner guidance. The cliff that the Fool stands on evokes the edge of our known world—and the leap of faith we need. It's a reminder that risk is essential to progress. Your task is to take these bright energies and make them work for you.

Meaning: Possibilities

You can manifest your own wonderful future. Every new journey starts with that first step, and The Fool encourages us to embrace the fresh starts and opportunities that life offers. Picking this card indicates you are absolutely correct to have a sense of faith and optimism. The Universe is guiding you on your path—have faith in your own abilities and trust that everything will unfold as it should. You are being reminded of untapped talents, ideas, and opportunities that you possess. You have the power to shape your own destiny and explore a wide range of options. Travel and dramatic life changes are well starred and can lead to personal growth and transformation. Be open to new things and willing to take risks. You can break free from stagnation. Trust in the process of life, and trust in the Universe. You are protected and supported as you embark on your new journey.

I The Magician

This is the most potent card of manifestation. The Magician stands before a table adorned with various tools and symbols. One arm is raised to the sky and the other points toward the earth, connecting the spiritual and earthly realms. The Magician is a conduit, with the power of alchemy to transform the spiritual into something real. On the table before the Magician are representations of the four classical elements: a cup (Water), a pentacle (Earth), a sword (Air), and a wand (Fire). The Magician possesses mastery over the elements and the ability to harness their power for creation and transformation. This card is associated with the number one, signifying beginnings, potential, and the power of transformation. The infinity symbol hovers above the magician's head, signifying the infinite potential and possibilities at the Magician's fingertips. It suggests that there are no limitations to what can be achieved with the right mindset and focus.

Meaning: Power

You have the power at your fingertips to manifest your desires and dreams into reality. Just as The Magician juggles the elements to transform, you have all the tools and experiences required to make your heart's desire come true. Your past has gifted you with insight and skills to take control of your destiny. Now is the time to put that knowledge to use. You are the master of your own fate, and your actions will determine the outcomes you desire. So seize the moment and channel your energy into action. Use your unique skills and talents to shape your world. Your power now is great— but remember true freedom comes from using your power responsibly and ethically. You are the creator of your own destiny. Trust in yourself and your abilities. Watch as your wishes become real on this earth.

Keywords: *Juggling, experience, fulfillment, control, freedom, action*

Mantra:

I am confident.

II The High Priestess

II The High Priestess
I trust my intuition

Keywords: *Insight, power, secrets coming to light, spiritual insight, mystery, knowledge*

Mantra:

I trust my intuition.

The High Priestess sits behind a thin curtain which is open and drawn to the side. The moon hovers above her head and next to her is a dish of pomegranates. On either side of her stand two pillars, marking the entrance to this sacred, mystical temple. The veil represents the boundary between the conscious and unconscious realms. It suggests that there are hidden truths, mysteries, and knowledge that lie just beyond our understanding. The moon reflects the feminine, intuitive, and emotional aspects of our psyche, as well as connection to divine cycles. The pomegranates are related to the Greek myth of Persephone, who ate six pomegranate seeds in the underworld, linking her to it forevermore—thus this fruit indicates a connection to the realm of the unconscious. The High Priestess holds a sacred book representing hidden knowledge, spirituality, and the pursuit of wisdom. The pillars represent duality and stability, and link with the number two, signifying balance and the feminine.

Meaning: Potential

Tap into your inner resources to unlock hidden knowledge and bring your desires into reality. Trust your instincts as you work toward your goals. Listen closely to the whispers of your subconscious mind; they hold the keys to manifesting your desires with precision and authenticity. You possess hidden reservoirs of power and potential. This power isn't necessarily loud or overt; it resides in your ability to access and harness the deeper realms of your consciousness. Be prepared for revelations that can lead to a deeper understanding of your life path. Meditation, prayer, or mindfulness will help you attain higher wisdom and gain clarity about your desires. In love, honesty will enable you to create the relationship of your dreams. Education can unlock greater success. You have the knowledge to make sound financial decisions; trust your instinct and keep your own counsel.

III The Empress

A woman with a starry crown and scepter in one hand sits on a throne, surrounded by lush vegetation, with a heart-shaped shield, bearing the Venus sign. The Empress is the third card, and the number three means abundance, fertility, and growth in numerology. The swell on her stomach indicates pregnancy, emphasizing connection to the cycle of life and birth. Her crown signifies rulership and authority over her realm. The round orb of her scepter symbolizes the Universe. The lush, green surroundings connect to the abundance of nature and the Earth's fertility and power. The Empress represents the motherly instinct to care for and protect those we love as well as creativity, ideas, and growth. It is within our unique power to make something new and wonderful.

Meaning: Creating

The energy of The Empress is surrounding you, bringing forth a period of creativity and prosperity. Just as the Empress nurtures the growth of life, you will find yourself in a position to cultivate and manifest abundance. Family bonds and relationships take center stage—there's a deepening of connections with your loved ones, bringing warmth and harmony. Your creative energies will also be flowing strongly, and ideas and projects flourish with ease. Art, business, or any form of self-expression have the potential to bear fruitful results. Nurturing opportunities will present themselves abundantly. You may find yourself in a position to care for others, offer support, or provide guidance. Embrace this role with an open heart, as your compassionate nature will have a positive impact on those around you. This card enables you to manifest a new project. A pregnancy or the creation of a new family member may be part of your future.

III The Empress
I am abundant

Keywords: *Femininity, family, pregnancy, nurturing, opportunity*

Mantra:

I am abundant.

IV The Emperor

The Emperor sits on a throne, wearing a suit of armor and a crown adorned with ram's horns, symbolizing his connection to Aries and the planet Mars. Behind the Emperor, a mountain range signifies aspiration and aptitude of command, while a small river at the foot of the mountains represents hope and the emotional side of The Emperor. He exudes a sense of authority and control over his surroundings. The Emperor's throne is made of solid stone, signifying stability and structure, a reminder that you need to establish a strong foundation and set clear boundaries. The Emperor's scepter symbolizes the ability to take control of your destiny and shape your reality. This card is associated with the number four, which in numerology terms is reflective of balance and stability.

IV The Emperor
I am in control

Keywords: *Masculinity, stability, security, ambition, power, authority, promotion*

Mantra:

I am in control.

Meaning: Structure

Taking on the role of a leader can enable you to manifest your heart's desire, as can firming up boundaries and adding more structure to your life. It's time to create a secure environment for yourself and those you love. You may need to make a decision—but once it is made you can see your way through to your ultimate goal. Present yourself with determination and moral authority. Promotions, achievements, and praise will be yours soon enough. Remember—you're in charge, you have the final say. It's time to take your place at the head of the table. You have the power and moral authority to settle disagreements now. There is the potential for achievement, success, and recognition now. Watch for mature and assertive masculine types who can help realize dreams in love, money, and career.

V The Hierophant

A spiritual leader, The Hierophant, is wearing robes and religious finery. The glowing crown is associated with ultimate authority, and also signifies the Hierophant's higher level of consciousness and mental link to a higher power. The Hierophant wears a blue scarf around his throat, which signifies speaking truth. The Hierophant's raised right hand and the two followers behind him show a connection to the divine or higher realms. The two pillars behind the Hierophant represent Law and Freedom. At his feet are five keys, which unlock spiritual knowledge and wisdom and he holds a pentacle design. The Hierophant is associated with the number five in numerology, which is all about change and growth.

V The Hierophant
I accept guidance

Meaning: Belief

Look to tried-and-tested routes to manifest your heart's desire. Real and lasting success is yours for the taking and established norms and social or cultural expectations can give clues to what path you should take next. Study and gaining knowledge will also be part of your path as true wisdom and knowledge is key now. Guidance may come from an authority figure, a mentor, a teacher, or a spiritual leader who plays a significant role in your life. Workwise, success will come from climbing up an established career ladder route rather than jumping into a risky venture. This is a time to look, not leap. In relationship readings, this card can indicate marriage and stable "forever" partnerships. If you're already wed, it heralds a deeper level of commitment in a romantic relationship. When it comes to money, invest in the tried-and-tested to expand your bank account rather than insecure new ventures.

Keywords: *Tradition, marriage, religion, faith, learning, seeking*

Mantra:

I accept guidance.

VI The Lovers

A man and a woman stand together, representing humanity in its original state of innocence. They are in the Garden of Eden: the Tree of Knowledge is on the left and the Tree of Life is on the right. The lush flowers and vegetation show the beauty you can reach when you live in a loving state. This is a card ripe with possibilities for manifestation. After all, unions are the beginning of creation. The Lovers card is associated with the number six, which stands for unconditional love and the ability to support, nurture, and heal.

VI The Lovers
I am supported by love

Keywords: *Harmony, relationships, partnership, alignment, unity*

Mantra:

I am supported by love.

Meaning: Choices

When The Lovers card appears, it's a reminder of the importance of being honest with our significant others and most importantly ourselves when it comes to building the foundations of our best future. It's also about choices. Two paths diverge, presenting you with a decision that could alter your course significantly. Weigh your options not just with logic, but with your heart, especially when two people are involved. Love can be the catalyst to overcome any challenge and push a cherished bond to new heights. In the realm of existing relationships, this card suggests a partnership that has the potential to become deeper and more profound, reaching greater levels of intimacy. However, the card advises that you may need to make a conscious choice now. Beyond love, The Lovers card has a broader implication. In the working world and business, you are contemplating a pivotal decision. Each path ahead represents different possibilities and realities—tap into your intuition to make the best choice. Moneywise, the card prompts you to ensure your investments are in line with your core values and principles. Invest in what you truly believe in and you will create the life you desire.

VII The Chariot

A driver steers their chariot with two horses—one black, one white. These creatures represent the dualities and conflicting forces within us, such as our desires, emotions, and intellect. To manifest effectively, you must find a balance between these opposing forces, aligning them toward a common goal. The charioteer moves forward, which signifies progress and forward momentum. The square on his chest represents the material world. The stars and crescent moons dance above him, reminding us of the connection between the material and spiritual realms. This card encourages you to stay in command of your environment and circumstances. The chariot is associated with the number seven, which signifies intuitive vision and spiritual progress.

Meaning: Will

The Chariot is a call to steer your own course toward your destiny—you have an inner belief that you have the right qualities to create a marvelous future. And you're absolutely correct. You're feeling determined and resolute. Receiving this card is a powerful omen, promising not just good fortune, but success that requires your engagement and drive. It's a time for focused action and sure-headed resolve. Commit to your course, and the rewards will be within your reach. In matters of the heart, should your relationship have gone awry, The Chariot advises a return to the proper track through deliberate effort. And if you're looking for love, this card is a klaxon to be proactive. Professionally, this card heralds a very promising phase: make bold moves! You can chase your goals with single-minded vision, swerving any diversions. Keep your eyes on the prize with determination, and you will thrive. Financially, The Chariot heralds serendipitous turns of fate, suggesting that taking the initiative in financial decisions could lead to positive outcomes.

VII The Chariot
I can find balance

Keywords: *Victory, will, self-assertion, control, discipline, progress*

Mantra:

I can find balance.

VIII Justice

VIII Justice
I make wise decisions

Keywords: *Fairness, truth, law, cause and effect, clarity, morality*

Mantra:

I make wise decisions.

A woman clad in red, which symbolizes passion, courage, and action, is seated on a throne. Her sword represents the power of reason, truth, and justice. It signifies the logical aspects of decision-making. The sword's sharp edge symbolizes cutting through illusion and falsehood to reveal the truth. The scales represent balance, fairness, and the idea of weighing options and consequences. They symbolize the need for objectivity in judgment and decision-making. The scales remind us that our actions have consequences, and that justice should be impartial. The sun and moon represent duality and the balancing of opposing forces. They remind us that justice seeks harmony. Justice is associated with the number eight, which in numerology is about balance, power, courage, and inner strength.

Meaning: Responsibility

The Justice card signals that it's time to focus on the significant decisions lying before you. It invites you to consider how your choices resonate with the Law of Attraction, reminding you that every decision sends out a vibration that will return to you in kind. This card is reminding you of fair judgment—call upon Justice to guide you to equilibrium in your affairs. If there's an injustice, this card assures you that the Universe is poised to restore what is right. It's an encouragement to ensure your actions are in line with your highest intentions. What you manifest will be in accordance with what you deserve. In relationships, if you've been pouring love and kindness into the partnership, expect joy and good times. In money and business, seek fairness, not only in how you treat others, but also in expecting it in return. When it comes to legal matters, a ruling will be made soon. Once the decision is made, it's important to accept and move on. Buying or renting a new home is likely as Justice is a strong indicator of signing a contract.

IX The Hermit

The Hermit is an old, hooded man standing on the top of a mountain, holding a lantern in one hand and a staff in the other. He looks like a solitary figure, but he is at ease with his isolation. The lantern symbolizes guidance, wisdom, and the search for truth in the darkness. To manifest our desires, we must first illuminate our own path through self-reflection and inner guidance. The staff represents spiritual authority and leadership. The mountain is a reminder of the challenges we must overcome on our spiritual journey. Climbing the mountain signifies the ascent to higher consciousness and understanding, which is necessary for successful manifestation. The Hermit's solitude and isolation represent the importance of introspection and self-reflection. It is associated with the number nine in numerology, which is all about introspection, solitude, wisdom, and spiritual enlightenment.

Meaning: Guidance

This card is about finding one's light within and using it to illuminate your path. The Hermit suggests that the answers you seek and the path you wish to manifest lie within your own inner-wisdom and enlightenment. So reflect on your personal goals and desires. By turning inward, you will find clarity and the right intention, setting the stage for attracting what you truly want. By focusing on spiritual development and inner wisdom, you boost your consciousness and ability to manifest. You become more aware of the bountiful opportunities the Universe presents, allowing you to move closer to your outcome. In love, solitude and going deep into your subconscious to purge any hang-ups will mean you can attract the right type of relationship. In career and money, you are reminded that riches and prestige are not the only markers of success. Focus on the highest good and the future of your dreams will fall into place.

IX The Hermit
I seek truth

Keywords: *Solitude, search, introspection, soul-searching, contemplation*

Mantra:

I seek truth.

X The Wheel of Fortune

X The Wheel of Fortune
I am flexible

Keywords: *Fate, change, cycles, destiny, karma, life's ups and downs*

Mantra:

I am flexible.

At the center of this card there is a golden wheel that appears to be turning. This wheel represents the cycles of life and the constant change we experience. It's a reminder that both good and bad times are temporary. An astrological glyph resides in each corner of the card, which represent the four fixed signs of the zodiac—Taurus (top left), Leo (top right), Scorpio (bottom right), and Aquarius (bottom left). These creatures symbolize the unchanging aspects of life amid the ever-turning wheel. They also correspond to the four elements, Fire, Earth, Air, and Water, highlighting the elemental balance needed for manifestation. An owl, representing knowledge and wisdom, sits on top of the wheel and on either side, there are butterflies signifying transformation and rebirth. The number 10 is associated with completion and endings.

Meaning: Luck

The message from this card is to trust in the cycle of change. The great news is that the Universe is working in your favor. This is a time to stay positive, maintain a clear vision, and trust that the Universe will rearrange itself to bring those opportunities and lessons that align with your highest good. In love, the Wheel of Fortune suggests a turning point. If you are single, you might soon encounter a significant other who profoundly impacts your life. If you are in a relationship, expect changes that will either strengthen your bond or lead to new insights and personal growth. Focus on the feelings and experiences you wish to have in your relationship and watch as this marvelous love grows. Financially, the Wheel of Fortune points to positive change, but reminds you to stay open to opportunities. In terms of career, it can be a harbinger of a promotion, a new job, or a change in direction. Make the most of the shifting energies and trust that your instinct is shaping your ideal work situation.

XI Strength

A woman holds the jaws of a lion, demonstrating her mastery but also her gentleness over this ferocious beast. The lion represents raw, primal energy. The woman's ability to control the lion with grace and compassion symbolizes the mastery of one's animal instincts and reflects the need to harness one's inner energies and desires. Above the woman's head is the infinity symbol, reminding us of the infinite potential of the human spirit. The woman's white robe symbolizes purity, spirituality, and the divine. The yellow background is indicative of joy, vitality, and the sun's energy. The crown signifies that inner strength and courage can lead to the manifestation of love, beauty, and positive experiences. A serpent is depicted eating its tail and encircling the woman and the lion, mirroring the cyclical nature of life, death, and rebirth. Strength is the 11th card and in numerology, the number 11 means intuition, enlightenment, and the connection between the physical and spiritual realms.

XI Strength
I have courage

Meaning: Courage

The Strength card reveals that inner grit and positive thinking are key to overcoming obstacles and attracting your desires. In terms of love, Strength indicates a phase of nurturing and healing. If you're single, it's a time to cultivate self-love and prepare for a relationship that cherishes your true worth. For those in relationships, it suggests strengthening bonds—remain strong yet tender. Financially, Strength encourages you to foster talents and skills to attract abundance. Tackle financial challenges head on with confidence, negotiate with wisdom, and remain true to your goals. In the workplace, this card represents influential leadership and personal power. It's about manifesting your goals by being assertive yet understanding. It might also suggest overcoming work-related challenges through endurance and moral courage.

Keywords: *Resilience, persuasion, influence, compassion, fortitude, inner power*

Mantra:

I have courage.

XII The Hanged Man

XII The Hanged Man
I am enlightened

Keywords: *Sacrifice, release, martyrdom, new perspectives, suspension*

Mantra:

I am enlightened.

A man hangs upside down from a tree by his ankle. The tree represents the Tree of Life and connects to the concept of spiritual enlightenment. The Hanged Man has a bright halo around his head, indicating enlightenment and a new perspective gained through his sacrifice. His garments are black and white, suggesting a balance between the physical and spiritual realms. His legs are crossed in the shape of the number four, which is associated with stability and foundation. It seems discombobulating as on first glance, he is quite comfortable looking at life from another angle—for now. This card is number 12, the number of completion, and the end of one cycle and the beginning of another.

Meaning: Insight

The Hanged Man signifies the need to release outdated patterns. It's a call to suspend action—momentarily at least—and reassess goals to make sure you are aiming for the right thing. For love, drawing this card is a suggestion to pause. If you are single, it might be time to let go of that list of must-haves and open yourself to the Universe's plan for you. In relationships, letting go of control and embracing vulnerability could lead to a deeper connection. In finances, this card indicates a new perspective or approach could be wise. Reappraise certain spending habits or investments that are no longer serving you. The Law of Attraction requires a clear and positive vision for wealth. So do your research and collect your thoughts. Then push forward with a plan. In the context of work, The Hanged Man suggests that now may not be the time for aggressive career moves. Instead, weigh up your goals and values. Are you chasing positions or projects that don't feel right for you? Authenticity is key when it comes to feeling fulfilled.

XIII Death

A skeletal figure cloaked in black reminds us of the universal and timeless nature of chapters ending, but also of transformation and new beginnings. In the background, you can glimpse the rising sun, which symbolizes hope and new beginnings. It reminds us that even in the darkest of times, there is the potential for renewal and transformation. At the feet of Death, there is a white rose, reflective of purity and rebirth; from death and decay, new life can emerge. The river signifies the flow of time and the journey of the soul. The process of transformation is never-ending and vital for growth and renewal. It's the 13th card, which in numerology means originality, transformation, and innovation.

Meaning: Renewal

This card marks the end of a major phase, making way for new opportunities. It represents the necessary release of old patterns, thoughts, and relationships to make room for new desires and intentions. It's about embracing change to manifest a new reality. Letting go of what no longer serves us can be a revolutionary act, opening ourselves up to attracting what we truly desire and need. For love, while the Death card can sometimes predict the end of a relationship, it may simply mean the close of a phase within a relationship. This ending is a marvelous opportunity for growth and the beckoning in of a more fulfilling partnership. Likewise with money, this card can mean the need to change one's approach. It might suggest letting go of an investment or attitude to finances that is no longer beneficial, opening the door to attract greater abundance. In terms of work, the Death card signifies significant shifts. Think changing jobs, careers, or even starting anew in a different field closer to your true passions. It's a reminder that, while change can be daunting, it is often necessary for true fulfillment.

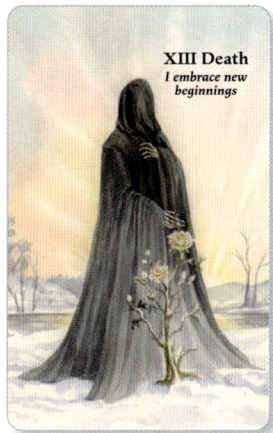

XIII Death
I embrace new beginnings

Keywords: *Endings, transformation, transition, letting go, metamorphosis*

Mantra:

I embrace new beginnings.

XIV Temperance

XIV Temperance
I create harmony

At the center of the card stands a graceful angel, with one foot on land and the other in water, symbolizing their ability to bridge the gap between different realms. The angel represents a divine messenger or intermediary between the physical and spiritual worlds. The angel holds a cup in one hand and a citrine crystal in the other, representing the harmonizing of opposing elements. Manifestation involves aligning your inner and outer worlds, making it easier to attract what you desire. In the background, a rising sun represents illumination, clarity, and enlightenment, and a constellation of stars represents the heights you can reach. The sign of Sagittarius is aligned with this card, and is a reminder to find peace within. The card is number 14 in numerology, representing fresh starts—you're about to embark on a new phase in life.

Keywords: *Moderation, patience, purpose, meaning, blending, combination*

Mantra:

I create harmony.

Meaning: Balance

When this card appears in a reading, it symbolizes harmony and taking a moderate approach. This is not a time for extremes: it's all about taking the middle road. In terms of love, Temperance indicates a time for patience and understanding. Both partners are learning to meld their differences and work together. If looking for a partner, a sensible approach and taking steps for self-improvement could be the answer. Embodying love and peace within oneself will attract similar energies. Financially, Temperance is a sign to moderate and balance one's approach to money. It advises against extreme decisions, suggesting that careful planning and patience will lead to gradual and stable prosperity. Set clear, positive intentions about finances and trust that the Universe will provide the necessary resources. In the context of career, Temperance calls for teamwork and cooperation for success. Discover a balanced approach to work and life, avoiding burnout. Nurture patience, consistent effort, and a positive mindset, and watch your dreams unfold beautifully.

XV The Devil

The Devil, a satyr-like creature, represents the material world and physical pleasures. A man and a woman are shown chained, but the chains are loose, implying self-limitation. Our beliefs and fears can trap us and hinder our ability to manifest our true desires. The pentagram represents spirit subjugated to matter—the physical world overpowering the spiritual, a warning against letting material concerns dominate one's spiritual growth. The Devil holds a torch, symbolizing illumination and destruction—in other words, understanding and embracing one's shadow side. The shadowy background represents ignorance and the unknown. Part of manifestation involves confronting these darker aspects. The Devil card is associated with the sign Capricorn and is number 15, representing individuality and change in numerology. It signifies the need to release old patterns and embrace transformation.

Meaning: Materialism

The Devil card serves as a reminder that when you focus solely on the material world or become obsessed with outcomes, you may inadvertently tether yourself to the very things you wish to avoid. It's time to liberate yourself! It's about breaking free from the illusions and chains of the physical world, using the Law of Attraction to manifest true happiness and reveal your highest self. Think of how you can free yourself from your own limiting beliefs and fears. In love, The Devil examines the chains that hold you back, whether they are obsessions, past hurts, or destructive patterns. Fostering self-love and releasing negative attachments can transform your love life for the better. For money and work, The Devil signifies a need to reassess your motivations. Are you working just for financial gain? Does your job fulfill you? You can't be enslaved by the materialistic aspect of work and wealth. Attract abundance by finding your soul's purpose.

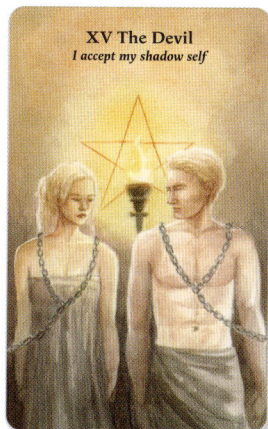

XV The Devil
I accept my shadow self

Keywords: *Bondage, obsession, hedonism, temptation, desire*

Mantra:

I accept my shadow self.

XVI The Tower

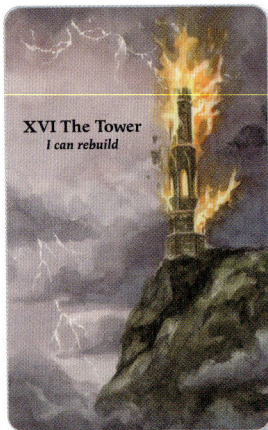

XVI The Tower
I can rebuild

Keywords: *Upheaval, breakdown, chaos, awakening, reckoning*

Mantra:

I can rebuild.

Atop a mountain stands a tower, against a dark and stormy sky. A lightning bolt has struck, rendering the tower ablaze. The bolt represents sudden, unexpected change. It's a symbol of destruction as well as enlightenment, striking the tower and signifying a moment of revelation or awakening. The Tower itself is a sign of ambitions, structures, or beliefs built on shaky foundations. Its destruction signifies the collapse of these unstable elements. The flames can indicate the burning away of old beliefs to make way for new growth. This card suggests that while change can be disruptive and even frightening, it's also an opportunity for growth and rebuilding on a more solid, truthful foundation. This card is number 16 and in numerology this represents new starts after upheaval.

Meaning: Sudden change

The Tower card is a sign of upheaval or a revelation that clears the path for new structures. It's a powerful reminder that sometimes, the old must be torn down to make way for the new. Drawing this card is a signpost that what you have been manifesting is coming to fruition in perhaps unexpected ways, often shaking the foundations of your world. It serves as a wake-up call, but as disruptive as it may initially feel, you'll see its worth when you look back. In love, The Tower could mean a sudden realization that dramatically changes the relationship—a breakthrough leading to a more honest and robust relationship. Be ready to rebuild more authentic connections. Regarding money, The Tower can forecast sudden changes in financial status, urging for a reassessment of how you attract and manage wealth. It might be a time to break free from financial constraints or thinking patterns. When it comes to work, expect significant shifts—maybe a change of career or an unexpected turn in your job that requires you to adapt quickly. Embrace the change! The Tower is clearing the way for new opportunities.

XVII The Star

A woman pours water onto the land and it flows into a lake. This act symbolizes nourishment and healing, suggesting the rejuvenation of the earth and the subconscious mind. A large eight-pointed star represents hope, inspiration, and guidance. The smaller stars symbolize chakras or energy centers, indicating a balance of energies. A bird sits on a tree, showing inspiration and a higher vantage point or perspective. The woman is clad in a white dress representing vulnerability and purity, signifying truth and the essential self, free from societal constructs. This card represents hope, faith, and a sense of boundless possibilities. The act of pouring water symbolizes the flow of emotions and the nurturing of desires into reality. This card suggests that after hardship, there's a renewal of optimism and a clear path toward achieving one's dreams. The Star is often associated with the zodiac sign Aquarius and its innovation, humanitarianism, and idealism. This is card 17, which in numerology can suggest that you are being called to take charge of your life in a way that is aligned with your spiritual path.

XVII The Star
I am inspired

Keywords: *Inspiration, generosity, serenity, renewal, clarity, optimism*

Meaning: Hope

A period of inner clarity and personal transformation beckons. Like the stars, your desires can light your path toward achieving your goals. Yes, you may have been through stormy times, but you are stronger, more resilient and can heal and move forward. If you've been through a rough patch in love, calm waters are ahead. You are open and able to create a relationship that is not only romantic but also deeply spiritual and nurturing. In terms of money and wealth, The Star indicates a time of abundance and prosperity is on the horizon. Continue working toward your financial goals and remain positive. For work, now is the time for creativity. Your unique ideas are likely to be recognized and appreciated. Kickstart projects or ventures, your qualities are attracting success!

Mantra:

I am inspired.

XVIII The Moon

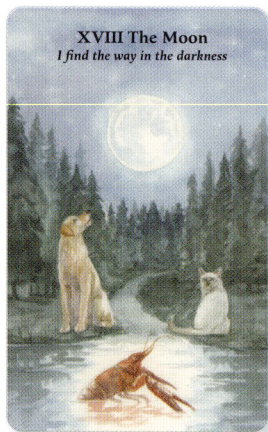

XVIII The Moon
I find the way in the darkness

We see a path that leads off into the distance. On either side stand a cat and a dog representing our animalistic nature—one is refined, and the other wild. The Moon shines down, a symbol of intuition, dreams, and the unconscious. Its light is dim, suggesting a world of illusion and ambiguity. A crayfish emerges from the water, representing the early stages of conscious awareness. The water is the subconscious mind, where dreams and memories reside. What you're trying to manifest might be vague. The path to realization is not clear, and intuition plays a significant role in guiding through the shadows. This card is associated with the astrological sign Pisces, known for its intuition, sensitivity, and connection to the spiritual realm. It is number 18 in the Tarot deck, reflecting hidden truths and navigating life's complexities.

Keywords: *Illusion, subconscious, intuition, uncertainty, doubt*

Mantra:

I find the way in the darkness.

Meaning: Ambiguity

The Moon card urges you to pay close attention to your instincts—they are messages from the Universe. The Moon speaks to the need for clarity in your intentions and beliefs—remember, like attracts like. In love, The Moon urges that you should look beyond illusions and see the truth of your relationship or feelings. Do you have the relationship that nourishes and feeds your soul? Step through confusion or misunderstandings, and you will be rewarded with the love you desire. Take a cautious approach when it comes to money. It's not the time for risky investments or taking leaps without planning or thought. Again, drill down to what it is you really want. Trust your intuition when making financial decisions and work toward wealth goals with a clear and honest intention. In the workplace, The Moon can indicate uncertainty and hidden truths. Do you truly love your career path? Is it really "you"? Understand what it is you truly seek and then move toward it, guided by your inner wisdom and intuition.

XIX The Sun

The Sun, a symbol of vitality, success, and optimism, beams down, indicating that things are illuminated clearly without shadows. A young girl with golden hair smiles and holds a flag, representing innocence, joy, and a successful new beginning. Sunflowers bloom in the background, symbolizing loyalty and longevity. They turn their heads to follow the sun, looking toward the light or positivity. In manifestation, this suggests aligning oneself with positive and life-affirming energies. A wall or barrier is shown in the background. This acknowledges the need to overcome obstacles or past limitations that one has moved beyond. This is the 19th card, and in numerology, this represents fresh opportunities.

Meaning: Enlightenment

Congratulations! It looks like you are on the precipice of achieving desires and the manifestation of good times. Expect great enthusiasm and energy being gifted to you by the Universe. Your positive mindset and continuous efforts are about to pay off. In terms of love, if you are in a relationship, The Sun is heralding a time of joy, celebration, and deeper bonding. Mutual understanding and shared visions flourish, bringing joy to your life. For those seeking love, The Sun's rays are guiding you toward a significant, blissful connection. Stay open and maintain a sunny outlook, as your radiant energy attracts equally vibrant partners. The Sun is an indicator of prosperity and abundance. Past efforts, coupled with a positive attitude, attract wealth and stability. It's a time for enjoying the fruits of your labor, with potential for investments to flourish. Keep focused and remain confident—you are entering a prosperous phase. For career and work, The Sun predicts a period of achievement and recognition. Your hard work, creativity, and leadership are noticed—expect promotions or successful completion of projects. Let your talents shine and welcome success.

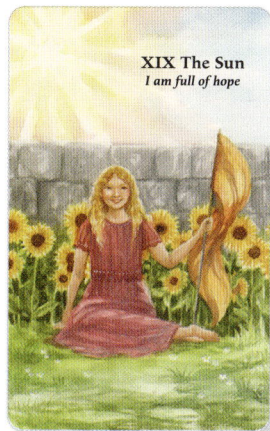

XIX The Sun
I am full of hope

Keywords: *Joy, success, celebration, positivity, vitality*

Mantra:

I am full of hope.

XX Judgment

XX Judgment
I know my destiny

An angel is blowing a trumpet—an awakening, a revelation, and an important call to action, the realization of one's true calling or destiny. The snow-capped mountains in the background represent challenges and the climb toward higher goals and aspirations. They reinforce the idea of overcoming obstacles. The water is emblematic of the subconscious mind and emotional clarity. It suggests that understanding one's emotions is crucial for effective manifestation. The card is number 20, which is also known as The Law of Attraction number because of its association with abundance and manifestation.

Keywords: *Judgment, rebirth, inner calling, absolution, resurrection*

Mantra:

I know my destiny.

Meaning: Evaluation

Drawing The Judgment card indicates that the past, present, and future are converging to reveal a significant turning point. It's a period of awakening, when you can start to act and live to your true purpose. In terms of love, Judgment predicts a period of evaluation. You're ensuring your partner is your true soulmate. For those seeking love, shaping a clear vision of the partner you desire can draw that person into your life. Financially, Judgment is a call to weigh up your financial strategies and decisions. Ponder on past investments and spending habits and make adjustments that are in sync with your long-term goals. This will bring clarity. Visualizing wealth and prosperity can attract the opportunities and resources needed to improve your financial situation. In your work and career, this card signifies a critical juncture. Does your job and pathway truly reflect your life's purpose? Pursue vocations that not only bring financial stability but also make you feel fulfilled and at peace. Manifesting your ideal job can happen now, as long as you keep true to your instincts. Remember, your career should not only pay for you to live, but also make your contentment and happiness grow.

XXI The World

The world appears inside an infinity wreath, which symbolizes wholeness, completion, and never-ending love. The realization of all possibilities being gifted to you by the Universe will bring joy. It signifies a moment of satisfaction as one cycle ends and another begins, underlying the continuous flow of life's journey. There are four representations of the elements (Water, Air, Fire, and Earth). The holistic understanding of these elements is crucial for effective manifestation. The World is the 21st card of the Major Arcana. The number 21 is connected to comfort, protection, and positive energy.

Meaning: Fulfillment

The World serves as a powerful reminder that your thoughts, words, and intentions have the potential to manifest tangible outcomes. It looks like your desires are in line with the Universe's abundance and your highest wishes and efforts are about to come full circle. If you're single, it suggests that you are about to meet someone who will complete you. For those in a relationship, it signifies that your love is thriving—it's likely that a significant milestone or the celebration of a shared achievement is on the horizon. It's a reminder that love, when nurtured with positive thoughts and actions, can grow and blossom in beautiful ways. Happily, The World predicts prosperity and abundance. Financial goals are coming to fruition, reflecting a period of stability and reward. Continue focusing on your objectives with positivity, as this will attract further abundance. Investments should mature, or you might receive recognition that leads to financial gain. This card also suggests the attainment of career goals. Your hard work and dedication are about to pay off, bringing you to a satisfying phase of your career. Recognition or an opportunity could arise that propels you to the next level. Embrace the future with gusto—the Universe is on your side!

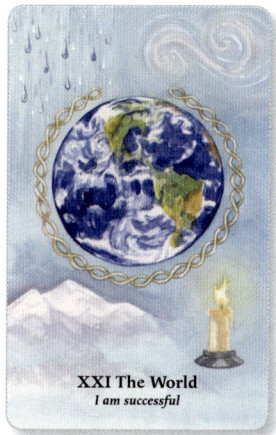

XXI The World
I am successful

Keywords: *Completion, integration, accomplishment, travel, involvement*

Mantra:

I am successful.

The Minor Arcana

In the Minor Arcana, each of the four suits is ruled respectively by one of the four elements—Water, Air, Fire, and Earth. Each element represents different facets of human experience, influencing our intentions, energy, and the Universe's response to our desires. Together, these elements offer an approach to manifesting and the Law of Attraction (see page 4), emphasizing the need for balance between desire, emotion, thought, and action. By understanding and integrating the lessons of Water, Air, Fire, and Earth, we can attract and manifest our deepest desires into reality.

The Four Suits

The four suits in the Minor Arcana are Cups, Swords, Wands, and Pentacles. Each suit contains 14 cards: 10 numbered cards, and four court cards—the Page, Knight, Queen, and King. Each of the suits represents a different area of your life:

CUPS

Element: Water
Emotions, intuition, love, feelings, relationships

SWORDS

Element: Air
Intellect, challenges, conflict, mind, decisions

WANDS

Element: Fire
Action, initiative, invention, travel, growth, energy

PENTACLES

Element: Earth
Work, money, home, long-term goals, family, health

Working with the Elements

Tarot readings and manifestation both start with the setting of intentions. In manifestation, you clarify what you want to bring into your life. In Tarot, you might ask a question to understand an aspect of your life better. So, before you start a reading, consider which element is most suited to your issue. Perhaps your question is about love, so Water/Cups is suitable, or a matter that requires courage (Fire/Wands). Maybe you need to find out about wealth (Earth/Pentacles), or you're feeling in need of clarity (Air/Swords). Before the reading, picture the relevant suit in your mind's eye. You could even trace the symbol of the suit with your finger on your hand before shuffling the cards for added power during a reading. You can read an in-depth explanation of each element and suit below.

Water, represented by the suit of Cups, is the realm of emotions, intuition, and connections. Water teaches us that to attract what we truly desire, we must first understand our deepest emotional needs and align our intentions with our emotional wellbeing. It emphasizes the power of visualization and feeling the emotional fulfillment of our desires as if they have already manifested, thus using the Law of Attraction to draw those experiences into our reality.

Air corresponds to the suit of Swords and symbolizes thought, communication, and intellect. Air emphasizes the significance of mental clarity, focus, and the power of our beliefs and self-talk. It reminds us that our thoughts and words are potent manifesting tools; by maintaining positive thoughts and expressing our desires clearly to the Universe, we can attract the outcomes we wish for. Air teaches us to cut through negativity and doubt, focusing on our goals and the steps to achieve them.

Fire is the element associated with passion, creativity, and action. In Tarot, it corresponds to the suit of Wands and embodies the spark of inspiration that motivates us toward our goals. Fire encourages us to ignite our desires with enthusiasm and to pursue our ambitions with courage and determination. It teaches that a strong will and positive action are key, reminding us that the energy we put out into the world is a powerful attractor of similar energies.

Earth is represented by the suit of Pentacles and is associated with materiality, stability, and practicality. It grounds us in the physical world and highlights the importance of taking practical steps toward our goals. Earth encourages us to embody our desires, to work toward our ambitions, and to trust that our efforts will attract tangible results. It teaches the value of patience, persistence, and understanding that manifesting is not just about wishing but also about doing.

The Numbered Cards

Each number in the Minor Arcana has an association that gives you more information about how to interpret the card. By looking at the associations of the numbers together with those of the suits, and any cards alongside, you can get more insight into predictions and meanings in a reading.

Aces (1, I):
Beginnings, initiative, drive, potential, and new opportunities

Twos (2, II):
Balance, partnerships, and dilemmas

Threes (3, III):
Interactions, teamwork, and communications

Fours (4, IV):
Rest, stability, and contemplation

Fives (5, V):
Conflict, challenge, and obstacles

Sixes (6, VI):
Growth, overcoming challenges, and clarity

Sevens (7, VII):
Faith, potential, confidence, determination, and patience

Eights (8, VIII):
Progress, reward, and change

Nines (9, IX):
Heightened energy and fruition

Tens (10, X):
Outcomes, completions, rewards, and consequences

The Court Cards

The court cards of the Minor Arcana can represent influences and symbolize people in our lives and individuals we come across.

The Pages can stand for youthful people, but also denote new phases and beginnings.

The Knights can indicate figures in our lives who are vigorous and brave, and reflect periods of activity and action.

The Queens embody wise, experienced figures in your life and are indicators of power, potential, and advice.

The Kings can signify authority and power, in the form of both people but also situations. They also point to drive and ambition.

Page of Pentacles
My curiosity opens the path to new growth

King of Swords
My decisions are guided by justice and truth

Ace of Cups

Keywords: *Love, romance, connection, creativity, birth*
Mantra: *I am loved.*

Celebrate new beginnings and joy. This is a time ripe for fresh starts, particularly in matters of the heart and happiness. New friendships can be sparked now, so open yourself to the opportunity to connect with new people as it might lead to wonderful developments. A truly fortunate time beckons for significant life events such as engagements and weddings. Social gatherings and parties can spark incredible experiences. Creative pursuits are charmed. Whether it's launching a business rooted in your passions or childhood aspirations, your projects are likely to flourish now. If you're employed, a promotion could be in the offing. Financially, some good news is winging its way to you.

Ace of Cups
I am loved

Two of Cups

Keywords: *Soulmates, partnership, friendship bonds being created, union, perfect harmony*
Mantra: *I cherish the bonds I form.*

The Two of Cups card heralds a period of celebration and the manifestation of love—the union of two energies, forging one bond. It's all about the synergy of mutual intention. When it comes to love, the seeds of intention you plant now have the potential to blossom into a beautiful reality. Single? A new love—if that's what you desire—will be on their way to you. In existing relationships, it's about cultivating respect and gratitude. Your thoughts and attitude can transform your partnership into something extraordinary, transcending the sum of its parts. If an old flame is on the scene, it might be time to open a new chapter. In the realm of business, the Two of Cups suggests that partnerships can thrive.

Two of Cups
I cherish the bonds I form

Three of Cups

Keywords: *Celebration, group, weddings, third-party situations, collaboration, relationship*
Mantra: *I have respect.*

Parties, good times, and bonhomie are all indicated by this card. The card also represents collaborations in the most wonderful sense—working with others will make things happen and beckon positive results and a sense of communal achievement. It's a positive sign for sharing emotions with close friends or family and finding support in these relationships. This card highlights strong bonds of friendship and community. It's about the joy that comes from shared experiences and mutual support among friends or community members. Looking for love? Don't turn down invites as you might meet a keeper! Couples will be enjoying celebrations, and good news at work and for family are all starred.

Four of Cups

Keywords: *Boredom, melancholy, comparison, dismissal, awakening*
Mantra: *I am open to new possibilities.*

Necessity is the mother of success—remember this if you're feeling a bit disillusioned now. You can transform weariness into realization. You're contemplating what's truly important to you, or you're considering a new perspective or approach to life. This card may indicate that you or your partner are feeling unenthusiastic about the relationship, or that there's a need to re-evaluate what you want from love and partnerships. In any situation, the Universe is asking whether you are missing the silver lining in a situation that seems uninspiring. Consider what it is you truly want. Once you've worked it out, ask for what you want directly— and see fortune flourish.

Five of Cups

Keywords: *Grief, sorrow, loss, sadness, emotional pain*
Mantra: *I learn from my losses.*

You could be experiencing regret or remorse over a past action or inaction, and the need to acknowledge these feelings but also to learn from them. While this card may represent disappointment and sadness, you shouldn't feel despondent at receiving it. Yes, there is a sense of loss, whether it's a relationship, an opportunity, or another significant aspect of life. There may be sadness, and it's okay to grieve for what has been lost. This card also carries a message of hope, representing new opportunities and the potential for emotional renewal, so shift focus from what's been lost to what remains.

Five of Cups
I learn from my losses

Six of Cups

Keywords: *Past-life connections, nostalgia, childlike joy, sweet memories, reunion*
Mantra: *Joyful memories enhance my present.*

There is a nostalgic glow to picking this card. Looking back on your childhood or reconnecting with someone from your past will bring joy. This card represents gifts, sharing, simple pleasures, acts of kindness, and the good times of childhood returning to your life. In love, childhood sweethearts could be coming back on the scene. For work, activities or professions connected with children and childhood, or something that brings out your inner child such as the creative arts, are key. If you had a secret yearning from childhood, you can manifest it to come true now. In finances, this card might remind you to be generous but not naïve.

Six of Cups
Joyful memories enhance my present

Seven of Cups

Keywords: *Illusions, deception, indecisiveness, overwhelm*
Mantra: *I make choices with clarity.*

This card represents choices, fantasies, and the illusion of plenty. It's a card that may appear in a reading when you're faced with many options—whether its jobs, lovers, or something else—leaving you unsure which to choose, or perhaps you're lost in wishful thinking and daydreams, potentially losing touch with reality. Your task is to distinguish between viable paths and unrealistic fantasies. If you're feeling overwhelmed with so many choices, this card is urging you to reach within to receive the right answer. Ground yourself and approach your decisions with a clear, realistic mindset. Once you're on the right path, envision your best future and take proactive steps to improve the situation.

Seven of Cups
I make choices with clarity

Eight of Cups

Keywords: *Walking away, abandonment, escapism, time to make a change, breakups, taking a break*
Mantra: *I seek deeper meaning and emotional fulfillment.*

Walking away is not a failure. This card is assuring you that cutting your losses can clear the way for new beginnings. You can move away from something emotionally meaningful due to a realization that it no longer serves your growth or happiness. This could be a relationship, a job, a belief, or even a long-held dream. Material or superficial gains no longer satisfy, and there's a quest for spiritual or emotional truth and fulfillment. You could need to pay homage to this. It's okay to feel sad, to soul-search. You're leaving behind old values or ways of life—what have you learned? Let this inform your new vision.

Eight of Cups
I seek deeper meaning and emotional fulfillment

Nine of Cups

Keywords: *Wish-fulfillment, overindulgence, dreams materializing, satisfaction*
Mantra: *I express gratitude for the abundance of love and happiness in my life.*

This is a manifestation card that can deliver your most heartfelt wishes. It's a wonderful card to receive and indicates pure joy. You're enjoying a sense of emotional wellbeing and happiness, and this card can signify a period of satisfaction in various aspects of life, such as relationships, career, or personal achievements. The job you have always hankered for, the right relationship, your dream house—these can all be delivered now. And if you're left in any doubt? Say it like it's already happened and be sure to count your blessings and give thanks to the Universe. Then watch your beautiful reality unfurl and enjoy.

Nine of Cups
I express gratitude for the abundance of love and happiness in my life

Ten of Cups

Keywords: *Long-term relationships, family-building, home, fairy-tale endings, achieving your desires*
Mantra: *I am surrounded by love and contentment.*

This card symbolizes a time of emotional satisfaction and finding happiness in your personal relationships. This is about the lasting long-term success and happiness we all aim for—a joy that is sustainable rather than flash-in-the-pan. It's indicative of a period of peace and harmony. After anguish, there's resolution, and with it a sense of unity. It's a beautiful indicator of happy family life as well as romance, engagement, marriage, or welcoming a new addition to the clan. Receiving this card reminds us to appreciate and cherish our loved ones. Acknowledge and be thankful for the blessings—and see this gladness grow and expand.

Ten of Cups
I am surrounded by love and contentment

Page of Cups

Page of Cups
I explore my emotions with curiosity

Keywords: *Expressing true feelings, affection, innocence, tenderness, good news, romance*
Mantra: *I explore my emotions with curiosity.*

Good news is coming your way! A creative pet project, romance, or other joyful project has some happy communication connected with it. This card can literally indicate a bright, young soul coming into your life—someone youthful in body or mind. This card is often associated with an artistic type. It suggests it's time to listen to your intuition and express your artistic and emotional aspects. To make your best future happen, it could be time to use beauty in your life to beckon it. An emotionally fulfilling relationship, proposals, a new friendship, and smashing interviews can all be part of the exuberant prophecy of this card.

Knight of Cups

Knight of Cups
I pursue my passions and dreams

Keywords: *Romance, charm, magnanimity, beauty*
Mantra: *I pursue my passions and dreams.*

You're following your heart, taking a leap in the direction of your cherished dreams, especially in creative or romantic ventures. Giving or receiving thrilling messages or proposals is very much part of the story of this card. As with all of the court cards, this card can represent a flesh-and-blood individual—in this case, it's a romantic dreamer, a poet, or an artist sweeping in and stealing your heart. It's time to write or create your own visionary future. In love, this can mean a whirlwind romance, a charming suitor, or a time when emotions are running high in a relationship. Ensure that how you're living aligns with your passions and dreams.

Queen of Cups

Keywords: *Psychic visionary, overwhelming emotions, melancholy, intuition*
Mantra: *I nurture my emotional self and those around me with compassion.*

With empathetic, compassionate, and nurturing qualities this card can represent a mother figure or a caregiver, someone who is deeply in tune with emotions, both her own and those of others—perhaps a relative, mature friend, or workmate who is looking out for you. Receiving this card can signify a time of emotional stability and can suggest tapping into your intuition or paying close attention to your dreams and inner thoughts. The Queen of Cups is often linked with a deep appreciation for beauty and art. The card can signify pregnancy, a nurturing relationship, or a time of compassion and caring, urging you to approach situations with empathy and understanding. Career-wise, caring jobs are well-starred.

Queen of Cups
I nurture my emotional self and those around me with compassion

King of Cups

Keywords: *Clarity, equilibrium, emotional maturity, devotion, compassion*
Mantra: *I lead with emotional balance and wisdom.*

The King of Cups is a supportive figure who offers guidance and understanding. He's often seen as a healer or counselor, someone who listens and empathizes. This card could be signifying someone who is like this in real life. Its appearance is also encouraging you to trust your strong intuition and know that the answer to problems is a creative approach. In love, this card can indicate the arrival of a trustworthy, loyal, and caring partner. It is all about a relationship where emotional support and understanding are prominent. In career, fair and caring leadership, a diplomatic approach, and taking a balanced and emotionally intelligent approach is the right way.

King of Cups
I lead with emotional balance and wisdom

Ace of Swords

Keywords: *Change-making, communication, clarity, truth, inspiration*
Mantra: *I embrace clarity and truth.*

The Ace of Swords card is about breakthroughs, clarity, and the power of truth. Tap into your intellectual power to make clear decisions, and slice through the noise to find the truth. Use your mind as a tool for achieving your goals and overcoming obstacles. You can gain fresh insight that cuts through the niceties to start up a new friendship, or conversely sever ties with someone who is no longer offering you positivity. This card can indicate a new beginning or project, such as writing a book, that has a lot of potential to succeed. In love, this card can indicate a romance with someone clever with words, or in a relationship it's signaling that you can work through any issues with honest and good-faith discussion.

Two of Swords

Keywords: *Confusion, crossroads, indecision, stalemate, limited communication*
Mantra: *I open my heart and mind to new perspectives.*

This card is challenging you to face a decision with honesty and openness, using both intellect and intuition to find the right path forward. It indicates you have been at a stalemate or impasse, where no progress can be made until a decision is reached. You have felt the situation has become stagnant. However, there is a moment of contemplation here—now is a time for reflection before making a move, and for ensuring you have all the relevant information required. One thing is for certain, something has to change. This could refer to a career dilemma or a love quandary, such as choosing between lovers or taking sides between a partner and family. Ultimately, you will need to take action and be decisive.

Three of Swords

Keywords: *Heartbreak, separation, despair, infidelity, love triangle*
Mantra: *I find strength and the courage to heal and move forward.*

The Three of Swords is an invitation to acknowledge and express sorrow as a step toward healing. It may represent a time of grief, sadness, or feeling betrayed. You might have to let go of a cherished belief or project. The card can represent a painful but necessary truth being revealed. If you're in a relationship, this can sometimes point to a breakup, a conflict, or some kind of separation. You may even discover that a lover is involved with someone else. Singles may have to face up to the fact that past wounds are holding them back. Ultimately, drawing this card can be liberating—the first step to moving on and making the happiness you deserve a reality.

Three of Swords
*I find strength and the courage
to heal and move forward*

Four of Swords

Keywords: *A much-needed break, rest, recuperation, solitude*
Mantra: *Peace of mind is my strength.*

The Four of Swords is the card of rest and relaxation. It signifies a period of rest or recovery after a time of challenge or turmoil. Whether in work or while you're making a decision, it's time to take a break, recuperate, and gather your strength. Find some peace after stress or illness. Taking care of your mental, emotional, and physical wellbeing is paramount and will allow you to make your dreams come true soon. In love, if singles have been rushing about searching for love on dating apps, it's time to take a hiatus. After a rest you will feel rejuvenated. For couples, this can mean you can spend some time apart—not a breakup necessarily, but just some breathing space. Then you can come together again.

Four of Swords
Peace of mind is my strength

Five of Swords

Keywords: *Pride, grave loss, defeat, gossip, suspicion*
Mantra: *I choose my battles wisely.*

The Five of Swords signifies conflict that ends with both parties feeling battered and bruised, regardless of who wins. One person may come out as the victor but at a great cost to others involved. This card represents a scenario filled with tension, disagreements, or conflicts. It can indicate a hollow victory, where the win comes at a significant cost, and is not worth the price paid to achieve it. It suggests a lack of fairness and integrity in dealings in work and money. In a love reading, this card suggests conflict, strife, and communication breakdowns, where one partner feels defeated or unheard. If you receive this card, its message is, if you wish to manifest good things, is this battle worth the cost, spiritually and morally?

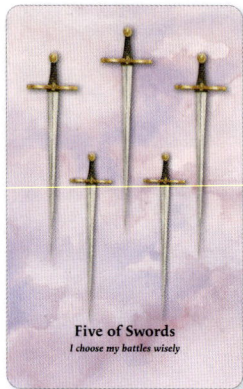

Six of Swords

Keywords: *Moving on, healing, relief, spiritual guidance, travel*
Mantra: *I leave behind what no longer serves me for a brighter path.*

The Six of Swords is a card of budding hope. There is transition afoot—healing and moving toward a more positive state after challenging times. You're finding your way from turbulence toward a calmer, more stable phase. This might not be easy, but it's necessary for growth and improvement. It suggests that while the wounds may still be fresh, the conditions are now right for healing and moving forward. Drawing this card can also mean travel or relocation, to bring about positive change or escape from negative circumstances. In love, this card represents a chink of light after a period of darkness. Relationship struggles are coming to an end, and singles are ready to work through issues that put a block on them manifesting the love they deserve.

Seven of Swords

Keywords: *Deception, lying, manipulation, dishonesty, scheming*
Mantra: *I navigate challenges with wisdom and discretion.*

The Seven of Swords asks if someone is trying to pull the wool over your eyes. This card may suggest that someone is being dishonest or using underhanded tactics. It warns you to be wary of deceit or to consider the consequences of not being completely transparent. Perhaps someone is not quite what they seem on first appearances. This card can also indicate the need for careful planning and strategy. Rather than facing problems head-on, a more subtle, strategic approach may be required. Be cautious in love, as you may not have the whole picture, and beware of your own white lies as they can become problematic. In terms of manifestation, it may be necessary to take the path less traveled, or manage a situation on your own terms.

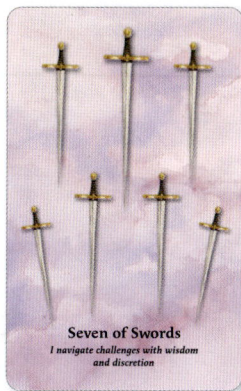

Seven of Swords
I navigate challenges with wisdom and discretion

Eight of Swords

Keywords: *Anxiety, over-thinking, embarrassment, slander*
Mantra: *I have the power to change my circumstances.*

This card is reflecting that you're in a situation of restriction, limitation, and feeling trapped, often by your own thoughts or circumstances that seem beyond your control. But the Eight of Swords contains an important message of hope and insight—the power to escape the situation lies within. You have a lot more capability than you're crediting yourself with. The limitations you face may be more self-imposed than real. It's time to think about your own beliefs and thoughts—could they be what's really holding you back? The solution to your problem is within reach, but you need to change your mindset to see it. In love, this card can indicate feeling trapped by a situation or relationship, but it's a reminder that there is no need to be passive—you are the captain of your heart.

Eight of Swords
I have the power to change my circumstances

Nine of Swords

Keywords: *Insomnia, mental anguish, fear, stress, self-doubt*
Mantra: *I transform worries into stepping stones for growth.*

Drawing the Nine of Swords is reflecting that you're experiencing anxiety, worry, and fear—the kind of stress that can consume a person when they are overwhelmed by negative thoughts or situations and can't sleep. Your mind is plagued by worst-case scenarios. One of the problems is that you're feeling isolated, like you can't face what you're dealing with, but you're urged to seek help and talk about what's troubling you rather than suffering in silence. The fact is, this state of mind is not permanent, and there are ways to manage and overcome these feelings whether they're about work or relationships. This card carries a message of hope. Facing one's fears is the first step toward overcoming them. Lighten the emotional load by seeking support from others.

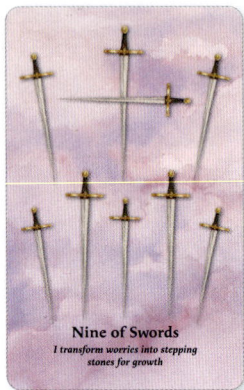

Nine of Swords
I transform worries into stepping stones for growth

Ten of Swords

Keywords: *End of a cycle, betrayal, martyrdom, change*
Mantra: *I acknowledge endings are necessary for new beginnings.*

The Ten of Swords is signifying a definitive closure to a situation. This ending is often unexpected and may be painful, but it marks the conclusion of difficulties or suffering. While it's true you feel let down by others and overwhelmed and exhausted, you will look back and see this moment as a gift, a moment of profound realization. Now the only way forward is up. Receiving this card is a reminder of the necessity of letting go of the past to make room for new beginnings. After the darkest night, dawn will come, suggesting that new opportunities can emerge from the ashes of the old. Accept the current circumstances as a necessary step toward transformation and healing. The end of one cycle paves the way for regeneration and growth.

Ten of Swords
I acknowledge endings are necessary for new beginnings

Page of Swords

Keywords: *Spying, high-alert, gossip, rebellion, immaturity*
Mantra: *I embrace curiosity and learning.*

The Page of Swords can represent a person in your life who is bright-eyed—curious, eager to learn, and full of ideas. It can also show that you're exploring new thoughts or perspectives, or the arrival of important news or messages, and you could be using your cleverness at work. This card can also reveal that you need to use clear communication to get your message and intentions across to the world. Let everyone know your thoughts and ideas clearly and be ready for honest discussions. Honesty and truth-seeking are important now, so be alert and aware of what is going on around you. You may need to cut through someone's deception. It's about being mentally prepared and able to defend your position or beliefs. In love, this card can indicate an intellectual relationship that sidesteps emotional intimacy.

Page of Swords
I embrace curiosity and learning

Knight of Swords

Keywords: *Rushing, knee-jerk reactions, hastiness, action*
Mantra: *I cut through obstacles in my way.*

The Knight of Swords can mean a literal person in your life—someone who is all about action and pushing ahead and doesn't mince their words. This card suggests that now is the time to pursue goals with determination and not to let anything stand in your way. Mental agility is indicated—think sharp thinking and clear communication. Use your intellect and words as tools to achieve your ends and fight for your beliefs, but make sure planning and research has already been done. There is the potential for conflict, aggression, or acting without thinking. This card can signify change that comes quickly. In love, communication will play a key role. The Knight of Swords could indicate a relationship where discussions and intellectual connections are prominent. Avoid harsh words or impulsive actions.

Knight of Swords
*I cut through obstacles
in my way*

Queen of Swords

Keywords: *Detached, logical, righteousness, composed, to-the-point*
Mantra: *I speak my truth with clarity and compassion.*

The Queen of Swords can mean there is someone in your life who uses their intellect and clear judgment in life, who can appear stern, but has a soft side underneath. In a reading this card may also signify a time when clear, unbiased thinking and communication are necessary. You or someone else in the situation has the qualities of the Queen of Swords—honesty, articulacy, and the ability to see through people's blather. So be like the Queen and think logically and objectively. Make decisions based on fact rather than emotion. If you're going through a tough time, use cool judgment rather than hot-headedness. In relationships, this card suggests that you value self-sufficiency at the moment, and shows you have high standards and are choosing to define boundaries with partners.

Queen of Swords
I speak my truth with clarity and compassion

King of Swords

King of Swords
My decisions are guided by justice and truth

Keywords: *Intelligence, seriousness, regal behavior, rationality, methodicalness*
Mantra: *My decisions are guided by justice and truth.*

The King of Swords can represent a person in your life with a sharp intellect and the ability to make clear, unbiased decisions. This person is knowledgeable and can provide sound advice. This card suggests that now is the time for clear thinking and communication. You want to be fair and make decisions objectively and from a balanced viewpoint, but it's also possible you can come across as a little critical and detached, so guard against that. In love, the King of Swords may signify a man of authority and action, such as a military type, and a partner who values clear communication and brains as well as physical attraction. Honest and open discussion can resolve issues within partnerships.

Ace of Wands

Keywords: *Bright future, new business or family, good news, possibilities*
Mantra: *I am a vessel for creativity and innovation.*

The Ace of Wands represents the start of something new. This could be a new project, job, relationship, or any kind of fresh start. It's a card that is all about seizing the day and pursuing opportunities that come your way. Now is the time to follow that creative spark—express yourself! You have the motivation and drive to put plans into motion. Naturally, this is a wonderful card to receive in relation to work, business, and new projects. With the right care and effort, something significant can grow. This, of course, can apply to love and new relationships, and is particularly fortuitous for pregnancies or making new additions to the family. Travel is another area where a journey can begin and open up to a fantastic adventure.

Ace of Wands
I am a vessel for creativity and innovation

Two of Wands

Keywords: *Partnership, letting go, new decision, forward movement*
Mantra: *I possess the power to shape my future.*

The Two of Wands is telling you to formulate a plan—the work is about to begin! Receiving this card indicates that you're standing at a crossroads with the world in your hands, contemplating your next move. An idea is being sparked and you're pondering your next steps. Do you stick with what you know or take a risk? Weigh up those options and consider potential adventures or investments. But ultimately, go with your intuition. You are in control over your destiny, so be encouraged to take charge of your future. Partnerships in business can grow something great, and in love, you are deciding whether to stay in the comfort of the known or explore new horizons. Your heart knows the answer.

Two of Wands
I possess the power to shape my future

Three of Wands

Keywords: *Manifestation, fruition, patience, traveling, opportunities arriving, teamwork*
Mantra: *I expand my horizons with every step I take.*

The world is at your feet! The Three of Wands is all about looking ahead and planning for the future. You know what you want and are starting to manifest your dreams. This card reflects the success that comes from persistence and effort. You are encouraged to continue your hard work, as it will lead to success. Life is expanding and you're ready to push your current boundaries and explore new opportunities. Those carefully laid plans are paying off. You've set a solid foundation and are now able to advance your ambitions and goals. Naturally, this card is a brilliant indicator for work and money. It also is indicative of freedom, adventure, travel, moving abroad, and foreign lands. In love, there is a foreign flavor— perhaps you'll meet someone from abroad, or have a destination wedding.

Three of Wands
I expand my horizons with every step I take

Four of Wands

Keywords: *Marriage, alignment, connection, a sense of belonging*
Mantra: *My life is a celebration of my achievements.*

This is a beautiful card to draw! It's associated with positive energy, harmony, and community. You're being told that you are coming into a period of happiness and stability, especially in your home life or close relationships. It's signifying a time of celebration, such as weddings, anniversaries, or other happy gatherings. You have accomplished something significant and now you can toast yourself and your loved ones with satisfaction. You're enjoying a sense of belonging to a group that shares your values. In love, this card signifies proposals or meeting someone at a get-together. More generally, it suggests homespun stability and security, especially in terms of home, family, and close friends. A new home, renovations, and housewarmings are all starred.

Four of Wands
My life is a celebration of my achievements

Five of Wands

Keywords: *Competition, disagreements, conflict, resistance*
Mantra: *I embrace challenges as opportunities to grow.*

This card is causing something of a stir. You might need to stand up for yourself, leading to a bit of friction and competition. Life brings us challenges and struggles from differing opinions and perspectives, and here we have a clash of egos or a conflict of interests. This card encourages you to stand your ground and assert yourself, but also to be strategic—this situation requires resolution. If you work in a competitive field, you could have to pit yourself against a rival, such as vying for a promotion or dealing with office politics or challenging group projects. Try clear communication to overcome these obstacles. In love, this card might indicate misunderstandings and a need to work through issues in an open way. Singles could be finding it challenging to find a partner who aligns with their values.

Five of Wands
I embrace challenges as opportunities to grow

Six of Wands

Keywords: *Victory, completion, celebration, accomplishments, moment of glory*
Mantra: *Success is my natural state.*

You're so close to accomplishment! Success, victory, and public recognition are within sight—yours for the taking. You have overcome challenges and obstacles and you're now in a position of achievement and acclaim. Understandably, your self-confidence is enjoying a boost and this positivity is manifesting a beautiful reality. It's a positive card—an affirmative answer in your favor if you are waiting on results or are in a legal tangle. You may be about to be feted in some way; if you're in a competition there should be good news coming your way. In finance and business, growth is likely. In love, your attractiveness is super-charged now, and couples should be savoring a win together very soon.

Six of Wands
Success is my natural state

Seven of Wands

Keywords: *Courage, negotiation, high-stakes situations, dedication to a path or project*
Mantra: *I stand my ground with courage and determination.*

Be ready to fight your corner. Your success and many talents have got you noticed by rivals. Be ready to stand your ground and defend beliefs or achievements against challenges or competition in a cool, collected, and resolute manner. It may be that you want to protect what you have created or achieved. This could involve safeguarding your reputation, your work, or your personal boundaries. You'll need to be assertive and strong in the face of opposition. Be determined and stand your ground—the presence of this card indicates you have the upper hand if you remain committed to your stance. Legal matters are indicated. In love this could mean fighting for romance or a principle.

Seven of Wands
I stand my ground with courage and determination

Eight of Wands

Keywords: *Travel, communication, quick changes, vitality, correspondence*
Mantra: *I am open to the flow of the Universe.*

Be on your toes! This card is all about rapid action, quick changes, and the swift approach of events—it looks like your dreams are going to manifest much more quickly than you anticipated. The Eight of Wands signifies receiving important information, propelling you to action. Your energies are directed like a heat-seeking missile toward achieving your goals. Travel could certainly be on your personal agenda. There should be positive news if you're searching for a new job or canvassing others for practical help. Watch out that money isn't flowing out as fast as it comes in. If you're looking to move, things should go smoothly and swiftly. In love, online dating can work for you, and existing relationships move fast.

Eight of Wands
I am open to the flow of the Universe

Nine of Wands

Keywords: *Roadblocks, pressure, persistence, test of faith*
Mantra: *Resilience is my key to success.*

Resilience, persistence, and the nearing completion of a challenge is the message of this card. You've been through a significant struggle and are now close to finishing this phase or project, but there's still one last challenge to overcome. It's a reminder to gather your strength, prepare for any final obstacles, and stand your ground. This card embodies the spirit of perseverance. Remain vigilant and determined. You have the inner grit and strength to overcome whatever stands in your way. Success is within reach if you maintain your resolve and continue to protect what you've worked hard to achieve. In love, this card shows that what you have is worth putting some effort into; taking steps to understand each other will lead to a relationship of greater depth.

Nine of Wands
Resilience is my key to success

Ten of Wands

Keywords: *Burdens, fatigue, stress, hard work, completion of a cycle*
Mantra: *I release burdens that do not serve me.*

This card indicates that you're carrying a heavy load, either literally or metaphorically, and you may be feeling weighed down by too many obligations or responsibilities. You may feel as if the Universe has given you more than you can manage. Are you pushing yourself too hard, trying to do too much on your own without asking for help or delegating tasks? The presence of this card is a gentle invitation to ask for help or reassess priorities. Make necessary changes to bring balance back into your life, whether that means finishing up projects or setting boundaries to protect your wellbeing. In love, you may feel like romance and relationships are just another responsibility. Make some me-time to take care of yourself— and then you will see the beginnings of the future you want.

Ten of Wands
I release burdens that do not serve me

Page of Wands

Keywords: *Courage, enthusiasm, impulsiveness, thrill, excitement, new ideas*
Mantra: *Curiosity and adventure guide me.*

A bright and breezy card! This could represent a person in your life who is enthusiastic, inquisitive, and full of vim. Is this you or someone you know? In more general terms, the Page of Wands suggests a time of exploring new ideas, passions, or even places. Expect a burst of creative energy or a newfound inspiration. Follow your curiosity and explore how it can lead to amazing things. This card can also mean a thrilling message or news that could be the catalyst for something very exciting. In terms of love, a person may enter your life like a mini whirlwind—an adventurous and inspirational type. This may be someone younger or from your youth. This will be fun, but not necessarily forever. Enjoy friendships with creative types who come into your life now.

Page of Wands
Curiosity and adventure guide me

Knight of Wands

Keywords: *Power, passion, energy, lust, adventure, an upcoming trip*
Mantra: *My actions are bold and fearless.*

Receiving this card can indicate that a swashbuckling type is about to enter your life, someone deliciously dynamic and adventurous. It also signals a time of enthusiasm and adventure. In career and getting ahead, you're ambitious, motivated, and hungry for new ventures. Travel, relocation, or a significant change in life direction are all possibilities raised by the Knight of Wands. There's the temptation to act on impulse and take risks without fully thinking them through, as well as a sense of restlessness. Like all gambles, don't forget your plan B. In love, this card represents exciting, whirlwind romances—someone charming and full of passion who comes into your life with a bang but may not be a keeper. Use the energies of this Knight to manifest the life you want!

Knight of Wands
My actions are bold and fearless

Queen of Wands

Keywords: *Ambition, confidence, lust, strong will*
Mantra: *Confidence and warmth radiate from me.*

This card may represent a fiery and confident woman who is focused and courageous, not a person to shy away from a challenge. This is someone you want on your team, who is pushing you ahead, encouraging you, and helping you create the world you want. If this is not an individual, it's a feeling—think high creativity and determination. You have the drive and energy now to turn visions into reality. Naturally, this is brilliant for business and financial growth. You can use your charm and intelligence to achieve your goals. Get out there and network. Expect good news and a busy time full of possibilities. In love, this is all about confidence and joy in relationships. Fertility is also indicated by this Queen.

Queen of Wands
Confidence and warmth radiate from me

King of Wands

King of Wands
I wield the power of leadership and vision

Keywords: *Authority, incoming changes, successful or prosperous future, leadership*
Mantra: *I wield the power of leadership and vision.*

A natural leader, who is assertive and direct and inclined to follow his own counsel, not the crowd—this could be someone in your life now, who is guiding and inspiring you. This card is telling you to embrace your unique qualities and act with confidence. Chase your passion and implement your ideas in real life. Enthusiasm and energy can propel you to positive change and success. When it comes to business and work, you see opportunities where others see challenges. Take the initiative! Be innovative! You could be making sudden decisions that surprise others. This includes in love, when someone who makes you swoon arrives in your life. Despite the speed things move at, this could be the real thing.

Ace of Pentacles

Keywords: *Successful investments, good fortune, inheritance, stable foundation, new job or business*
Mantra: *New opportunities for abundance flow to me effortlessly.*

Expect your goals to manifest into marvelous reality, especially those related to the material world. This card is all about turning ambitions into reality, particularly in career or physical possessions. Naturally it signifies new beginnings in business, investments, or financial ventures. It welcomes new prosperity and wealth, providing the opportunities are cannily pursued. While there is a strong monetary emphasis on this card, it can also mean abundance and prosperity in the form of resources or opportunities. Relationships and general wellbeing should be good. Feel a flush of optimism and trust in the natural process of growth and development. Efforts started now should flourish.

Ace of Pentacles
New opportunities for abundance flow to me effortlessly

Two of Pentacles

Keywords: *Bringing balance, releasing stress, transition, ups and downs*
Mantra: *I gracefully balance my responsibilities.*

It looks like you have become something of a juggler. You are balancing multiple responsibilities or priorities and trying to maintain equilibrium in various aspects of your life, be it work, finances, health, or relationships. You're adaptable enough to balance everything in a way that is sustainable for now, but there could be a need for re-evaluation to avoid future stress or burnout. Look at the big picture while weighing matters up. Can money and energy be better used? We always need to be aware that unexpected expenses can occur, and simultaneously maintain a growth mindset, so continue to be adaptable while looking after your most important asset—yourself.

Two of Pentacles
I gracefully balance my responsibilities

Three of Pentacles

Keywords: *Solid foundation, alliance, planning, long-term goals*
Mantra: *Collaboration brings shared success.*

Many hands can achieve much! Collaboration, teamwork, and skill in life and work that requires a coming together of talents and graft are highlighted. Anyone studying should see this as a very fortuitous message, as it shows that determination, dedication, and commitment should motor you to the top. This card also signifies building on success or foundations. You may not be the complete finished product yet and there is nothing wrong with acknowledging this and taking a position of curiosity and modesty. Soak in new knowledge and garner skills for future accomplishment. Hard work, determination, dedication, and commitment will get you where you wish. If you're working toward something, you should get what you're aiming for.

Three of Pentacles
Collaboration brings shared success

Four of Pentacles

Keywords: *Feeling closed off, conserving, materialism, control*
Mantra: *I manage my resources wisely, ensuring prosperity.*

You're holding on to something. This card is asking you why. An abundant philosophy requires you to give to the Universe in order to receive. So, what is holding you back at the moment? Receiving this card is a great blessing because it allows you to change gears and reassess your attitude. On one hand, your affairs are in order with a solid foundation; however, a conservatism or inner fear is blocking necessary growth. You are overly attached to something, be it money, an asset, or social status. The truth is, greater prosperity and good times are more than possible, so negotiate and smooth over any disagreements about investments with others and watch the good times roll.

Four of Pentacles
I manage my resources wisely, ensuring prosperity

Five of Pentacles

Keywords: *Rejection, loss, lack of resources, struggle*
Mantra: *I open the door to new opportunities.*

Money may be about to become a precious resource to you. This card is alerting you to an unforeseen expense. Life may feel like a bit of a struggle—but remember, this is a temporary thing. In career, there's a general feeling of being unsupported. Perhaps you need to seek help or reassess your financial or career path. Even if you suspect there is nobody willing to give you help, look closely. It's there, perhaps in the form of moral support from friends or family, financial assistance from the government, or even random acts of kindness from strangers. The trick is to accept and recognize it. The tough times will pass, and it will happen sooner by counting your blessings and cultivating a growth mindset.

Five of Pentacles
I open the door to new opportunities

Six of Pentacles

Keywords: *Shared wealth, combining finances, philanthropy, support, unity, community*
Mantra: *Generosity and receiving are in balance.*

A card of generosity and positive karma. The dark days are over and you are moving to a sunnier place in life. Now you may be in the position to help others—to pay back kindness or even to pay it forward. This help could be financial, but it might also mean sharing knowledge, time, or skills. If you're on the receiving end of someone else's generosity, accept help with grace and understand the balance of give and take. Financial stability in the form of gifts, grants, or loans is highly likely. It's all about being part of a community and helping each other out. In work, this card indicates being well-supported, and in love, generous and equitable partners are enhancing your life.

Six of Pentacles
Generosity and receiving are in balance

Seven of Pentacles

Keywords: *Investments, patience, long-term growth, commitment, stability*
Mantra: *Persistence in my efforts will yield security.*

After the hard work comes the rewarding moment when you can pause, look to see what you have done and what you have earned, and allow yourself a moment of satisfaction. And if you can't see it, is there still an obstacle to overcome? You should be smiling at drawing this card, as success is just around the corner! Be patient and keep going. You will soon be able to harvest your bounty. Naturally this is great for work and money, and can be applied to cherished plans and ideas, ambitions, or goals. In love, you will soon be able to manifest the future you desire, and this is also a positive card for health and wellbeing—it's encouraging you toward your goal.

Seven of Pentacles
Persistence in my efforts will yield security

Eight of Pentacles

Keywords: *Hard work, apprenticeship, discipline, diligence, mundane routine*
Mantra: *Dedication to my craft brings mastery.*

Through hard work and dedication, your skill and expertise are being honed. When this card appears in a reading, it can indicate a period of diligent work and improvement, where you are putting in a lot of effort to perfect your skills or produce something of high quality. It's a wonderful sign for a student to receive as it indicates you are becoming more professional and an expert in a field. It's also a positive card for anyone considering taking up a new course of study or training to improve their professional skills or personal interests. To manifest more of what you want, working hard will lead to success. In relationships, this card shows you're both on track to reach mutual goals.

Eight of Pentacles
Dedication to my craft brings mastery

Nine of Pentacles

Keywords: *Independence, entrepreneurship, achievements, freedom, wisdom*
Mantra: *I am surrounded by abundance.*

Receiving this card indicates financial stability and abundance. You have worked hard to achieve your goals and are now enjoying the fruits of your labor. Plans that you have been working toward are coming good. Savor the moment. Naturally for money and career, this is a beautiful harbinger. For love too, the Nine of Pentacles emphasizes the benefits of a stable and harmonious relationship. For single people, it might mean feeling content and at one. Ready to meet someone, but equally at ease as an independent operator. Moreover, this card is revealing to you how much you can find fulfillment in your own achievements and to rely on your own resources. You have the power to create a comfortable and secure life for yourself.

Nine of Pentacles
I am surrounded by abundance

Ten of Pentacles

Keywords: *Generational wealth, unexpected financial windfalls, security, prosperity*
Mantra: *I am building a lasting legacy of wealth and wellbeing.*

A fabulous card to receive, the Ten of Pentacles represents abundance in its truest sense, not just in financial wealth, but also contentment, often linked to loved ones. Perhaps long-term financial planning is paying off. It's time to celebrate! The achievement of success and stability in your life is indicated, particularly in the material or financial sense. Happiness and security beckon. This is a point of accomplishment, the culmination of a long journey, especially in a career or financial context. You might like to think about laying the foundations for your future security, whether through investments, property, or setting up structures for future generations. In relationships, this card points toward deep and enduring commitment and love.

Ten of Pentacles
I am building a lasting legacy of wealth and wellbeing

Page of Pentacles

Keywords: *Good news, learning, setting goals, loyalty*
Mantra: *My curiosity opens the path to new growth.*

This card is the personification of good news! It can represent a person who is eager to learn new skills and gain knowledge. They are ambitious and focused but also principled. A period of study and education could be on the horizon, and this card shows you'll possibly be embarking on new studies or training. The life you want can be realized through learning, and new opportunities abound in the realms of finance or education. A new project or venture has the potential to be very beneficial, and will boost your prosperity, so feel confident. You can realize your ambitions if you approach them with realism and commitment. There is good news on jobs, house sales, and money. Relationships can be renewed, and this card encourages you to reveal your feelings.

Page of Pentacles
My curiosity opens the path to new growth

Knight of Pentacles

Keywords: *Reliability, stability, patience, slow but steady progress*
Mantra: *I advance toward my goals.*

Knight of Pentacles
I advance toward my goals

We all want the Knight of Pentacles on our team. A person who is dependable, steadfast, and committed to their duties and obligations is or is about to be important in your life. Success will come through steady effort, perseverance, and a down-to-earth approach. Take a realistic view of situations and you can discover practical solutions to problems. There's a focus on financial stability and security, signposting you to patience. Long-term planning and foresight are required. You're advised to take the long view in business and money to create future wealth. And in other spheres, such as health and relationships, you will be able to create your ideal future. Slow and steady wins the day.

Queen of Pentacles

Keywords: *Promotion, opulence, luxury, pampering*
Mantra: *Caring for myself and others enriches my life with abundance.*

This card is signaling that a mature female or feminine person who is generous and usually wealthy or financially independent could be in your life now, mentoring you and giving good advice. She is a marvelous and warm presence—and she's on your side. It's possible she is a business partner. In a more general sense, you should be cheered that you have the ability to get what you want by taking a grounded approach. Set goals and work toward them steadily. There is growth in business, money, and love. Someone could come into your life and open up a brilliant new world. New family additions, marriage, and moves to green and leafy places are all possible interpretations.

King of Pentacles

Keywords: *Grounded energy, power, wealth, discipline, benevolence*
Mantra: *Ambition guides me to manifest prosperity and stability.*

The King of Pentacles represents an individual, potentially an older man, who is successful, wealthy, or influential, and often involved in business or finance. They are reliable, efficient, and have a knack for managing material resources. This card indicates financial stability and success, a time of prosperity when financial projects are successfully completed. It can also imply that you are in a position to enjoy the finer things in life, thanks to your graft and hands-on approach. If you have a challenge to overcome, this card reminds you that you're strong and confident with considerable resources of your own. It's indicating that recognition and pay rises should be on the way. In love, look out for someone with the King of Pentacles' qualities—he could be very good for you.